THE CHALLENGE OF BEING BAPTIST

THE CHALLENGE OF BEING BAPTIST

Owning a Scandalous Past and an Uncertain Future

Bill J. Leonard

BAYLOR UNIVERSITY PRESS

Cover Design by Andrew Brozyna, AJB Design, Inc.

Library of Congress Cataloging-in-Publication Data

Leonard, Bill (Bill J.)
  The challenge of being Baptist : owning a scandalous past and an uncertain future / Bill J. Leonard.
     p. cm.
  Includes bibliographical references (p.   ) and index.
  ISBN 978-1-60258-306-1 (pbk. : alk. paper)
  1. Baptists--Doctrines--History. I. Title.
  BX6331.3.L47 2010
  230'.6--dc22
                                        2010005249

To students at the Divinity School, Wake Forest University, 1999–2010,
whose energy and riskiness shaped a new school in its first decade.
With deepest gratitude.

CONTENTS

1

PREFACE
What's in a Name?

❈

It has been already seen, that the claim, for the church and for the conscience, of freedom from all human control, was a distinguishing and characteristic trait of the Baptists in former reigns. The divine saying, "FAITH IS THE GIFT OF GOD," moved, animated, strengthened them. Its practical assertion brought them into collision with every form of human invention in the worship of God.

Edward Bean Underhill, 1847,
describing seventeenth-century Baptists[1]

It was the order of the day (though I am sorry to say it) that we were constantly followed by a certain set of proselyting Baptist preachers. These new and wicked settlements were seldom visited by these Baptist preachers until the Methodist preacher entered them; then, when a revival was gotten up, or the work of God revived, these Baptist preachers came rushing in, and they generally sung their sermons; and when they struck the *long roll*, or their sing-song mode of preaching, in substance it was "water!" "water!" "you must follow your blessed Lord down to the water!". . . Indeed, they made so much ado about baptism

by immersion that the uninformed would suppose that heaven
was an island, and there was no way to get there but by *diving*
or *swimming*.

Peter Cartwright, nineteenth-century Methodist[2]

Our old name was confusing to many people. And the word
Baptist? A lot of people think that Baptists are very legalistic
or that Baptists are political. We are not any of that. We're a
nondenominational, Bible-believing church.

Brad Powell, pastor of Northridge Church,
Plymouth Township, Michigan[3]

If the name Baptist was good enough for the first "Baptist"
preacher to be called "the Baptist" by the Holy Spirit, it ought to
be good enough for us today. Many churches are dropping the
name "Baptist" in order to separate from the Biblical distinctions which have identified us with a particular body of faith. By
doing so, they must compromise their doctrine to accommodate the very people whose forefathers have persecuted the true
church down through history! This is a "trampling under foot"
the blood of millions who gave their lives for the faith.

Neuse Baptist Church, Raleigh, North Carolina[4]

In many respects, the people called Baptists always seem in transition. Congregational polity, individual conversion, biblical
interpretations, and doctrinal intensity provoked unity, diversity,
and schism from the beginning of the movement. In fact, Baptist
identity has often been a way station for persons who then moved
on to other religious communions. Former Baptists are to be found
among the early Quaker, Universalist, Unitarian, Shaker, Oneida,
Mormon, Restorationist, Adventist, and Pentecostal movements.
In the quest for the true New Testament church or the clearest biblical revelation, Baptists have not always remained Baptist.

More recently, however, Baptist identity itself seems to be perched on the edge of oblivion, with individuals, congregations, and denominations revisiting, ignoring, or uncertain about the nature of Baptistness as a viable tradition for the future. As a student of Baptist history, I am increasingly invited to address such questions as "Why would anyone want to be a Baptist?" "What are the best reasons for remaining Baptist?" and "Does the name Baptist hurt more than it helps?" This book is one attempt to address those questions by examining certain distinguishing marks of Baptist identity with particular attention to past approaches and current confusions. It explores classic Baptist approaches to polity, Scripture, conversion, and mission as they have impacted a Baptist witness in the church and the public square. My hope is that it will be helpful to those who confront the permanent transition that seems to have fallen on innumerable religious institutions throughout the world.

Numerous programs and projects facilitated this study. Some of the research was done for a conference on "Synodality" (church polity) held in Bruges, Belgium, at which I was the only Baptist representative. That gathering, composed primarily of European and American Catholic scholars, highlighted the sectarian messiness of Baptist theology and polity in contrast to older establishmentarian traditions. Other research grew out of preparations for an address given at the celebration of the two hundredth anniversary of the British Baptist Historical Society meeting in Prague, Czech Republic. Once again, European colleagues offered helpful responses to my reflections on Baptist identity. The three chapters of the book that deal with biblical hermeneutics, conversion, and ecclesiastical sacramentalism were initially produced for the Parchmen Lectures at Truett Theological Seminary, Baylor University. Reflections on the shape and future of Baptist identity began with research for addresses presented at gatherings sponsored by the Associated Baptist Press and the Cooperative Baptist Fellowship.

Baylor colleagues Beth Barr, Mikeal Parsons, and Douglas Weaver contributed to my understanding of the breadth of Baptist beliefs when we worked together on the volume *The Acts of the Apostles: The Baptists' Bible*, a work that highlights diverse interpretations of texts in the book of Acts from the seventeenth into the twenty-first century. Students at the Divinity School, Wake Forest University, comprised a community of scholars who let me explore these ideas in lectures and class discussions that formed and re-formed the content. I would also like to thank *Perspectives in Religious Studies*, who allowed me to reproduce part of my article "An Audacious Witness: Charting the Baptist Future One More Time" (vol. 36, no. 4, 2009, 477–89) in the final chapter of this book.

1

BEING BAPTIST
Scandalous Past, Uncertain Future

On the eve of the American Revolution, Anglican parson Charles Woodmason described the carryings on among the people called Baptists in the "Carolina backcountry." He wrote,

> They don't all agree in one Tune. For one sings this Doctrine, and the next something different—So that people's brains are turn'd and bewildered. And then again to *see* them Divide and Sub divide, split into parties—Rail at and excommunicate one another—Turn (members) out of one meeting and receive (them back) into another. And a Gang of them getting together and gabbling one after the other (and sometimes disputing against each other) on abstruse Theological Questions . . . such as the greatest Metaph[ys]icians and Learned Scholars never yet could define, or agree on—To hear Ignorant Wretches, who cannot write . . . discussing such Knotty Points for the Edification of their Auditors . . . must give High offence to all Intelligent and rational Minds.[1]

Parson Woodmason was as correct as he was condescending. Indeed, many contemporary observers would concur that Baptists continue to give "high offense" in the church and the public square.

In the United States, for example, when a Virginia congressman calls Americans to intensify immigration laws in order to keep out Muslims who might be elected to high office and might take the oath of office on the Qur'an, did he not just have to be a Baptist?[2] When members of a stem family church in Kansas staged protests at the funerals of soldiers killed in Iraq and shouted that such deaths are the result of God's judgment on the nation, did they not just have to be Baptists?[3] And what of the preacher who prayed that God might enable the death of President Barack Obama? He was, predictably, a Baptist.[4]

And then there are all those internecine "Baptist battles" fought incessantly in the pew and the press. For decades Baptists in the nation and especially the South have debated issues related to the inerrancy of the biblical text, ordaining women to Christian ministry, control of Baptist-related schools, academic freedom, secularism in the public schools, private school vouchers, trips to Disney World, *glossolalia* (speaking in tongues), praise choruses, baptizing homosexuals, rebaptizing Presbyterians, salvation for Jews and Muslims (or not), the "rapture" (before, during, or after Christ's second coming), drinking wine at communion or at dinner, and the gospel benefits of something called "Christian heavy metal" music. So-called worship wars divide congregations over issues related to the nature of preaching, liturgy, prayer, and praise. In other Baptist contexts schism arises out of conflicts over congregational and ministerial authority and debates over the role of clergy and laity.

Such divisions are not new, by any means. Early Baptists split over theologies of Calvinism and Arminianism, Sabbath-day worship, and the laying of hands onto the newly baptized. Later on, deep rifts developed over slavery and abolition, segregation and integration, and the role of women in church and pulpit. While some of its leaders helped form the Social Gospel, others opposed it vehemently. Theological differences continue, covering a wide spectrum from liberal to conservative, creating rifts over classic

Christian doctrines from the nature of salvation to the use of the King James Version of the Bible. Cooperation becomes impossible because convictions cannot be bridged.

Today, Baptists' missionary and benevolent programs feed the hungry, clothe the naked, and preach the gospel to rich and poor across the world. Some congregations bearing the Baptist name are among the largest in America. Others reflect membership that is stagnant or in rapid decline. Nonetheless, as the largest Protestant communion in the United States, Baptists represent a significant segment of the religious population. Amid their theological and cultural diversity, Baptists churches and individuals now confront a serious identity crisis as they anticipate the future. For all the public and private bombast in their denominations and churches, an increasing number of Baptists could not care less about the label *Baptist*, its history, and its traditions.

This book examines elements of the Baptist past as a way of informing current ecclesial dilemmas and future prospects for a Baptist future. It explores some of the most identifiable character-istics of this messy coalition of people who first claimed an iden-tity as a believers' church over four hundred years ago. It focuses on issues related to conscience and conversion, baptism and Bible, polity and globalism in an effort to discover ways in which Bap-tist identity might be reexamined, reformed, and reaffirmed at a time when many are questioning its validity and relevance. It is an attempt to revisit Baptist history through certain topics that were present from the beginning but seem to grow more complicated as the twenty-first century deepens.

Reshaping Identity: Baptists and Cultural Contexts

Early Baptists thrived in a religious culture in which dissent and diversity seemed the order of the day. The church was aflame with a variety of new religious movements that were driving old establishments to distraction. Seventeenth-century England was a seedbed of upstart Protestant communities that included Puritans,

Separatists, Independents, Presbyterians, Baptists, Quakers, Ranters, Levellers, Diggers, Seekers, Millenarians, and assorted other religio-political dissenters who were accordingly jailed, fined, exiled, and even executed by a government fretful that sectarian chaos would undermine political stability.[5] And it did. Amsterdam, the scene of Baptist beginnings around 1609, was itself a sanctuary for assorted individuals and groups that fled the dangers of their homelands in search of a modicum of personal safety and religious tolerance.

The Challenge of Pluralism

These diverse religious communities anticipated the modern denomination, articulating their own versions of New Testament Christianity often repackaged as fresh revelations or old orders revivified by the Holy Spirit, the church replaced or renewed. Baptists and Anabaptists (Mennonites and others) bumped into each other in Holland, anticipating the Free Church Tradition with its call for conversion and religious liberty, profoundly reshaping a second generation of Reformation churches, ideas, and practices.

With their emphasis on democratic congregational polity, conversion, theological diversity, biblical orthodoxy, and freedom of conscience, Baptists seemed poised for success or disaster in the modern world. In many ways they did succeed, especially in the West. In England they became a relatively small but significant nonconformist communion. In North America they thrived, a dissenting sect that by the early nineteenth century had become one of the largest denominations in the New World. A Baptist presence was evident in Europe by the mid-1800s, developing a notable community in Eastern Europe and Russia by the early twentieth century. Baptist mission endeavors, begun in the late eighteenth century, led to the founding of churches in Africa, Asia, and South America, many of which are thriving to this day. In fact, the missionary movement was an early impetus for collective endeavors that shaped the initial stages of Baptist denominationalism.

As the twenty-first century dawns, Baptists, like other Protestant denominations, confront new challenges brought on by the postmodern religious world. Denominational coalitions that took shape in the seventeenth and eighteenth centuries now seem in permanent transition if not outright decline. While historic traditions continue, they seem increasingly less viable as ways of organizing religious communions, at least in the West. Protestant sectarianism remains, evident in storefront churches, emerging churches, megachurches, and other independent congregations. Some of these congregations have taken on their own denominational style, sending out their own missionaries, publishing their own literature, and, in some cases, consecrating their own bishops.

Pluralism and religious liberty bring multiple religious groups into the public square. Contemporary pluralism extends to other world religions, New Religions, various types of syncretistic spirituality, and a rising secularism that often ignores religion altogether. While old ecumenical relationships continue and doctrinal divisions remain significant within Christianity, new areas of interfaith dialogue and increased "switching" from denomination to denomination, religion to religion seem the order of the day.

Conscience and Conviction: Baptist Divisions

Amid concerns for cultural pluralism, interfaith dialogue, and religious liberty, differences over faith, doctrine, and ideology remain. And debates over conscience and conviction do matter. Religious pluralism does not require conformity to a nebulous syncretism in which all beliefs must neatly fit together and divisions do not occur. Through the power of conscience individuals assert a commitment to a variety of beliefs, many of which contradict or challenge the beliefs and practices of others. Ideas regarding Scripture and tradition, faith and reason, God and gospel still galvanize religious individuals who know little or nothing of the ancient debates present at the Council of Nicaea, the Marburg Colloquy, or the Westminster Assembly. Divisions over biblical inspiration, Christology, and a variety of socioethical issues characterize Christian communities in general and Baptists in particular in churches throughout the world. And some religious beliefs cannot be reconciled. One Baptist's religious convictions may be another's heresy. Religious freedom offers the possibility that persons or groups may appear obnoxious to others when they voice their deepest convictions in the marketplace. In certain religiously volatile areas of the world doctrinal or interfaith differences continue to create the possibility of armed conflict and even death. And such divisions will not soon be ended. Indeed, they may create extended controversy and schism in the postmodern church. While religious harassment exists freedom of religion is much more normative now than in seventeenth-century Baptist life.

And divisions have taken their toll. When twenty-first-century Baptists "divide and Sub divide, split into parties, rail at and excommunicate each other,"[6] not just in the "Carolina back-country" but on CNN, would not any self-respecting believers want to distance themselves from their Baptist origins as quickly as possible?

The Name "Baptist": Retained or Relinquished

Some are attempting to do just that. For many contemporary churches, individuals, and denominations, even the name Baptist is up for grabs. A growing number of Baptist churches across the theological spectrum from conservative to liberal are (implicitly or explicitly) reexamining what it means to claim the name Baptist and whether to retain it in the years ahead. The reasons for individual or congregational distance from the name Baptist also reflect the times. Some have become convinced that "brand-name" religion no longer attracts persons as it once did. Many new congregations or "church starts" are founded as nondenominational fellowships or community churches even if they demonstrate characteristics of the Baptist tradition or have minimal affiliation with Baptist denominational groups. Some traditional Baptist churches have excised the name, at least from their public advertisements and Web pages, moving away from sectarian distinctiveness and appealing to a broader constituency. In 2008, one old-guard American denomination, the Baptist General Conference, born of Swedish immigration to America in the nineteenth century, officially changed its public name to "Converge Worldwide," retaining the name Baptist General Conference only "in some settings and for legal purposes."[7] Saddleback Church, the California-based megacongregation in which Rick Warren serves as pastor, has affiliation with the Southern Baptist Convention but does not use the name Baptist in its publications. Its Web page recounts the history of the church without any reference to its Baptist connections.[8]

Others suggest that the name has become so synonymous with division, dispute, and schism that it pushes persons away from churches instead of welcoming them. Some persons shy away from Baptist identity because they seem so shrill in their public disputes. Certain churches have simply lost any real sense of Baptist identity by default, having given limited attention to their history for years. They are historically Baptist, but few of their younger members know why or really care. In fact, in many cases new members choose such churches because of their particular approaches to ministry, worship, and service rather than the specific denominational name they bear. Ignorance is no excuse, however. Truth is, elements of Baptist identity may be more important than ever in offering responses to twenty-first-century religion and culture.

Beyond Denominations: New Forms of the Church

Baptists are also shaped by numerous ecclesiastical trends evident in the global Christian community. These new forms of the church are present in movements old and new, traditional and nontraditional. First, nondenominationalism is challenging traditional denominational systems across the world. Nondenominational community churches and fellowships claim ever-increasing constituencies, even as many traditional congregations relinquish or minimize denominational commitments. A global charismatic movement impacts theology, mission, and worship across the denominational spectrum, fostering a more "generic" form of Christianity that often distances itself from old-line sectarian attitudes and divisions. While denominations continue, they are no longer the only or even the primary ecclesiastical game in town. Denominational "switching," long present in America, seems at an all-time high even as denominational systems downsize, decline, or fragment. In short, fewer religious Americans think of their primary identity in terms of a denominational identity.

Megachurches, now approaching their third generation, continue to set agendas as major forms of the church nationwide. Megachurches are congregations of several thousand members, guided by a pastor/CEO/authority figure (and his or her family members), providing specialized ministries for target groups and organized around intentional marketing techniques. These large communions are in many ways minidenominations, offering in one congregation many of the ministries—education, publication, mission, and identity—previously provided through denominational systems. New stages of the megachurch movement have led some congregations and pastors to franchise themselves, utilizing state-of-the-art technology to export their ministries into congregations old and new, spread across the country. In some settings, the Sunday preacher is a hologramic image, downloaded from the "mother church," a phenomenon that gives new meaning to the term Real Presence. Megachurch models now have a massive presence in Korea, Ghana, Kenya, Nigeria, and other developing countries. Some megacongregations in this country and elsewhere promote a so-called "Prosperity Gospel," promising health and healing less as miracles than as entitlement to Spirit-baptized believers.[9]

One of the great unstudied issues in American religion is the impact of megachurch ecclesiology on African American congregations. African American megachurches are establishing a wide variety of educational and worship experiences, minimizing or competing with old denominational networks, and often developing new forms of economic entrepreneurial endeavors. A growing number of Baptist and Pentecostal clergy, especially in African American churches, are seeking consecration as bishops. In America these days, almost no one wants to belong to a denomination, but everyone wants to be a bishop!

More recently, in the United States and England, the Emerging Church Movement has appeared, challenging old ecclesial styles and megachurch agendas considerably. In their study of the movement, Eddie Gibbs and Ryan K. Bolger write that

> emerging churches are not young adult series, Gen-X churches, churches-within-a-church, seeker churches, purpose-driven or new paradigm churches, fundamentalist churches, or even evangelical churches. They are a new expression of church. The three core practices are identifying with the life of Jesus, transforming secular space, and commitment to community as a way of life. These practices are expressed in or lead to the other six: welcoming the stranger, serving with generosity, participating as producers, creating as created beings, leading as a body, and taking part in spiritual activities.[10]

Their leaders are rethinking the nature of Christian community and ministry itself, with the pastor as the "guide on the side not the sage on the stage." Much is made of the impact of varying aspects of postmodernism on the movement in contrast to older models shaped or still captivated by modernity and Enlightenment Rationalism.

Given these transitions, missiologist Wilbert R. Shenk concludes,

> The quest for authentic expressions of the Christian faith in Asia, Africa, Latin America, and the Pacific Islands on the part of the so-called younger churches is having a 'reflective" impact

on the West as well. The modern concept of theology as univer-
sal theological knowledge independent of ecclesial context has
been weighed in the balance and found wanting.[11]

And then there is the question of Baptist identity worldwide.
Outside the United States, Baptists occupy global minority status,
impacted by such diverse religio-cultural influences as the rise of
the European Union and the collapse of the Soviet Union, char-
ismatic-oriented spirituality, and northern/southern hemisphere
theological differences. In a new and very fine volume titled *Eastern
European Baptist History: New Perspectives*, edited by Baptist theologians Sharyl Corrado and Toivo Pilli, Corrado asks enduring historic questions in response to the permanent transition that has
descended on European Baptist groups, and most Christian communions worldwide. Corrado writes,

> What does it mean to be a Baptist? How do Baptists differ from
> those of other confessions or faiths? How does the Baptist tradi-
> tion in Eastern and Central Europe relate to what is called by
> that name in other parts of the world? How have Baptists his-
> torically understood themselves as part of the state and society
> in which they lived?[12]

Corrado notes that changes in Eastern European religio-political
life have led to questions of "identity" and "ambiguity" for Baptists
in the region. Their book explores many key themes that, while
applied to Eastern Europe, could describe a renewed quest for a
global Baptist identity. These include the need for "international
cooperation and influence among the worldwide Baptist family"
and the impact of "cross-denominational influence on the historical
Baptist movements." Corrado and Pilli conclude by asking, "How
does Baptist self-identification correspond to the identity bestowed
upon them by a secular society, and how should Baptists respond to
such misrepresentations and stereotypes?"[13]

Baptist Identity: Revisiting Historic Issues

As if these realities were not challenging enough, Baptists in America, especially in the South and Southwest, confront dilemmas born of the confluence of theology and culture that create unending controversy and division. First, it is clear that Bible Belt Baptists are losing their hegemony over the culture, numerically and perhaps theologically. Religious pluralism inside and outside the church now offers multiple choices for new generations of spiritual consumers. Recent concerns, many raised by Southern and National Baptist leaders regarding statistical declines or stagnation, illustrate that old demographics and new religious paradigms can have an impact on even the most orthodox of traditions. In other words, biblical inerrancy cannot stall demographics forever.

Second, Baptist appropriation of transactional conversionism has had a significant impact on the theology of a believers' church, often minimizing mystery, awe, and wonder in the salvific process. Instead of offering assurance of salvation, such transactionalism often fosters considerable doubt as to the validity of one's "eternal security," creating a religious culture in which Baptist church members claim multiple conversions and corresponding rebaptisms. Third, in some Baptist contexts, conversion has become the primary "outward and visible sign of an inward and spiritual grace," often minimizing the power and practice of believers' baptism and the Lord's Supper. Indeed, in many congregations, baptism and the Supper are almost afterthoughts, commandments or "ordinances" to be carried out but stripped of their spiritual depth and communal meaning by enduring influence of Old Landmarkism and Enlightenment Rationalism. Fourth, lack of theological clarity regarding conversion and baptism has left many Baptist churches uncertain as to the biblical and historical reasons for the baptism of children and the nurturing of children to and through faith both before and after the baptismal experience.

In fact, it appears that contemporary Baptist churches, especially in the American South, are confused, uncertain, or silent as to a clear theology of conversion, baptism, and rebaptism. The latter issue is perhaps the most pressing, a crisis exacerbated by the influx of nonimmersed but long-term Christians who seek membership in Baptist churches and the phenomenon of the rebaptism of Baptist church members who continuously reprofess faith and receive immersion multiple times. Many of these rebaptisms are administered to individuals initially baptized as children but who insist that they did not fully understand that action and request a new baptism after a more mature, genuine, or adult experience of faith. In responding to these varied phenomena, many Baptists have developed a "cut and paste" theology and practice without serious consideration of the biblical and historical implications of their actions.

Given these transitions in contemporary and postmodern theology and practice, how might Baptist history inform identity in the present and, more importantly, the future? As the twenty-first century deepens, aspects of the Baptist past are worth considering, whether churches or individuals use the infamous "B" word in their public statements or not. Rather than excise or exorcise all remnants of Baptistness from the ecclesiastical past, however, are there segments of that heritage worth acknowledging that continue to inform the future? To own the best contributions does not require claiming the entirety of Baptist history, nor does it mean scrambling to find something worth retaining in order to be historically correct. Rather, congregations could be intentional about revisiting the Baptist past with appropriate research before jettisoning the movement uncritically.

Baptist Praise and Worship, a hymnbook utilized by British Baptists, contains a hymn titled "By Gracious Powers," written by German theologian Dietrich Bonhoeffer in January 1945, only months before his execution by the Nazis. Its poignant verses include this profound prayer:

If once again, in this *mixed world*, you give us;
The joy we had, the brightness of your sun,
We shall recall what we have learned through sorrow;
And dedicate our lives to you alone.[14]

Twenty-first-century Baptists occupy a mixed world, a mixed church, and, in many cases, mixed families where multiple cultures and ideologies blend and collide. Baptists the world over are at once collegial and confrontational, scholarly and pragmatic, spiritual and worldly, diverse and uniform, with miles to go before they sleep and with questions of their future and their identity yet to be answered.

2

HISTORICAL CONSCIOUSNESS AMONG BAPTISTS
Owning and Disowning a Tradition

Not at the Jordan River,
But in that flowing stream.
Stood John the Baptist Preacher,
When he baptized Him.
John was a Baptist preacher,
When he baptized the Lamb,
So Jesus was a Baptist.
And thus the Baptists came.[1]

For some Baptists, past and present, that bit of nineteenth-century doggerel illustrates one popular response to a sense of historical consciousness. It reflects a powerful and enduring theory of Baptist origins, the Old Landmark belief that Baptists antedate all other churches through a historical lineage stretching directly to Jesus' immersion by John in the river Jordan. As one frontier preacher was said to have remarked: "Well, they didn't call him John the Presbyterian, now did they?"

In its most basic sense, the belief that a succession of Baptist churches extended all the way to the New Testament was a perfect paradigm for Baptists in their often desperate search for identity and historical connectedness. Having no single founder who looms large over their ecclesiastical landscape—no Luther, Zwingli, Calvin, or Wesley, no George Fox or Ann Lee—Baptists have long struggled with their historical and theological location within the Christian tradition. Were they Calvinists or Arminians? Were they missionary or antimissionary? Were they Protestants or simply New Testament Christians?

Not only do Baptists differ over their origins, but they also disagree as to the meaning of history and their place in it. These differences are particularly evident in the American South. In that region of the United States, Baptists' historical consciousness was shaped by such traditional paradigms as southernness, denominationalism, separatism, and Conversionist spirituality. Those themes helped Baptists organize identity in the past and the present. However, new transitions in the life and culture of the South and its churches are reshaping Baptists' historical consciousness significantly. In many cases, the collapse of these paradigms creates a certain historical confusion as to what it means to be a Baptist at all. This particular study surveys those early themes and reflects on the way current transitions impact historical consciousness.

Baptist Presence in the South

African American and Caucasian Baptists in the South constitute the largest regional Baptist presence in the world, numbering somewhere between twenty and twenty-five million persons. These Baptists demonstrate multiple consciousnesses exemplified in various groups and subgroups. In addition to the Southern Baptist Convention (SBC), that denomination which claims numerical, if not ideological, hegemony over the region, Baptist subgroups in the South include Appalachian sectarians, African American Liberationists, and Independent Baptist Separates. Each of these communions manifests intriguing, often contradictory historical consciousnesses in response to events past, present, and future.

The SBC is the largest Protestant denomination in the United States, claiming some seventeen million members. While its strength remains primarily in the South and Southwest, its influence and constituency are spread throughout the nation. Founded in 1845 as a result of the controversy over slavery, the SBC created a powerful programmatic identity for its people, a spiritual and regional legacy closely connected to southern cultural and social consciousness. The convention linked local churches, regional associations, and state conventions with a national system of boards and agencies that facilitated programs in education, missions, publication, historical studies, annuity, and other benevolent activities. The denomination funds six theological seminaries, sends out missionaries at home and abroad, and articulates its "modified Calvinist" theology in a confession of faith known as the Baptist Faith and Message. Since 1979, divisions in its ranks over biblical inerrancy, women in ministry, homosexuality, and denominational control have produced several new Baptist groups including the Alliance of Baptists, the Cooperative Baptist Fellowship, and Baptists Committed.

Primitive and Old Regular Baptists are perhaps the best known of some ten or more Baptist subdenominations in the central Appalachian region. Sometimes inappropriately labeled as "hyper-Calvinists," these Baptists grew out of the antimission movement of the nineteenth century as articulated in the "Black Rock Address" of 1832. Taking their cues from that antimission document, many mountain Baptists, as they are sometimes called, eschew Sunday schools, seminaries, revivals, elaborate denominational networks, and direct evangelism. They believe that they preserve "old-timey" Baptist ways in mountain churches, as evident in the "sacryments" of river baptism, closed communion, and "feet-washing."

African American Baptists in the South are associated with multiple denominations including the National Baptist Convention, Inc.; the National Baptist Convention, Unincorporated; the Progressive National Baptist Convention; and the American Baptist Churches of the South, a largely African American segment of the

American Baptist Churches, USA. In the South, many of these congregations were central to the Civil Rights Movement. A number of their pastors entered the public square to address issues of poverty and politics, voting rights, and community development.

Independent Baptists originated in the early twentieth century, with some churches splitting away from the SBC and others forming as new Fundamentalist-oriented congregations. These Baptists are strongly committed to Fundamentalist principles, often summarized in the classic "five points," including biblical inerrancy, Christ's virgin birth, as well as his substitutionary atonement, bodily resurrection, and literal second coming. Although antidenominational, they formed a variety of loose-knit organizations such as the Southwide Baptist Fellowship, the Baptist Bible Fellowship, and the World Fundamentalist Fellowship.

What makes each of these diverse groups discernibly Baptist? A brief summary of common ideals must suffice. First, they are all Biblicists, affirming the centrality of Scripture as the primary authority for faith, belief, and action. They demonstrate a variety of hermeneutical approaches to the interpretation of authoritative documents in approaches that take them in a variety of theological, political, and liturgical directions. Second, they are Conversionists who insist that all members of the church must acknowledge an experience of God's grace made known by personal faith in Christ. Third, they are "deep water Christians," in Will Campbell's words, immersionists who administer baptism by "dunking" to all who profess faith and seek membership in the church. Fourth, they are covenantal Congregationalists, constituting believers' churches centered in congregational autonomy and polity.

Baptist Origins: The Theories

Any study of Baptist historical consciousness must begin with a survey of the standard theories, oft-debated by Baptist scholars and church folk, as to the origins of the Baptist movement itself. Historians have long noted the presence of various theories of origin in Baptist historiography. In his classic work *A History of Baptists*, historian Robert Torbet documented three such theories. The first he labeled the "Jerusalem-Jordan-John" hypothesis, that effort to trace Baptist churches in unbroken succession back to the New Testament community and Jesus' baptism at the hands of John the Baptist. This successionism was an attempt to establish Baptists as the one true church, existing from the first century, not through apostolic succession but through a series of apostolic churches, dissenting, evangelical, persecuted, and Baptist in everything but name. Successionists generally claimed Montanists, Novatianists, Donatists, Albigenses, Waldensians, Anabaptists, and other sectarians as part of the Baptist family.

One dominant successionism was known as Old Landmarkism, a theology and historiography set forth by J. R. Graves (1820–1893) of Tennessee and J. M. Pendleton (1811–1891) of Kentucky. Pendleton's work, *An Old Landmark Reset*, written in 1856, marked the beginning of the movement that promoted Baptist churches as the only true New Testament communities "marked" by issues of closed communion, alien immersion, and the absolute autonomy of every congregation. Formally and informally, Landmarkism shaped Baptist ecclesiology throughout the South well into the twentieth century. Although lacking historical veracity, this theory became a popular method by which some Baptists promoted their orthodoxy as the true, indeed only, New Testament church.[2]

A second approach Torbet called the "Anabaptist Spiritual Kinship" theory, which sought to establish links between the seventeenth-century Baptists and the Radical Reformers of the sixteenth century. The idea of "kinship" reflects a disagreement among historians as to whether direct links between Baptists and Anabaptists can be established. Clearly, the two groups shared many of the same ideals—believers' church, believers' baptism, and congregational authority, among other things. British Baptists in the Netherlands began alongside the Anabaptists, though not directly out of their communities. Baptists contacted the Dutch Mennonites regarding

many subjects, especially the question of believers' baptism.[3] Yet
early Baptists also sought to distinguish themselves from the Radical Reformers. One seventeenth-century Baptist confession of faith
was composed by a group of Baptist believers, who noted that they
were "(falsely) called Anabaptist."[4]

A third idea of origins dominates Baptist historiography and is
called the "Puritan Separatist" theory. This view suggests that Baptist groups—both Arminian and Calvinist—grew out of segments
of English Puritanism, particularly the Separatist tradition. The
General or Arminian Baptists who constituted history's first Baptist
community in 1609 were a group of English Separatists in exile in
Amsterdam. Their Baptist identity took shape as they broke with the
Separatists over infant baptism and constituted a believers' church
grounded in a profession of faith followed by believers' baptism. The
Particular or Calvinist Baptists originated in London in the 1630s
as part of a congregation of Puritan Independents known to historians as the Jacob-Lathrop-Jessey Church. Particular Baptists first
instituted believers' baptism by immersion in 1641, affirming basic
Baptist beliefs within the context of Reformed theology.[5]

Historical Consciousness—Popular Identity

The three theories are symbols of Baptists' struggle for a greater
consciousness of origins and identities. As denominations took
shape and denominational competition increased, Baptists found
themselves in need of a clear historical identity that would distinguish them from Methodists, Presbyterians, Lutherans, and other
Protestant groups whose founders and origins seemed much more
discernable. Old Landmarkism became a vehicle for distinguishing
a particularly precise and classic history of Baptists. Landmarkism
was a popular theory of history that permitted Baptists to draw a
direct linkage with Jesus and the church of the New Testament by
tracing themselves across history through a succession of dissenting,
antiestablishment sects. Its history was essentially false, concocted

to provide historical identity in competition with other burgeoning American denominations and to prove that Baptists indeed constituted the truest of the true New Testament church. Landmarkism was people's history, appropriated by a variety of Baptist groups. It was an early Baptist response to denominational competition and debates over the nature of the true church.

The name Landmark was taken from Proverbs 22:28, which reads, "Do not remove the ancient landmarks that your ancestors set up," and was developed by Baptist leaders Graves and Pendleton. In 1854 Pendleton addressed the issue of whether pedo-Baptist ministers (from churches that baptized infants) should be allowed to preach in Baptist churches. He concluded that they should not since their churches were "societies," not participants in the true New Testament church. Landmark beliefs revolved around the following affirmations:

- Baptist churches are part of a succession of congregations that are "Baptist in everything but name," traceable from the New Testament era to the present.
- Baptist church practices were kept alive by dissenting congregations in every age since the New Testament period.
- Dissenting communions included Montanists, Donatists, Paulicians, Waldensians, Anabaptists, and Baptists.
- Landmarkists insisted that the kingdom of God is inseparable from the local congregation; that the only form of the church is the local, visible congregation; that only local congregations have the authority to administer the ordinances of baptism and the Lord's Supper.
- Baptists were not Protestants since their heritage predates the Reformation.
- Landmark churches administered the Lord's Supper only to members of that specific congregation; Landmark churches required the immersion of persons not previously baptized in a Baptist church. This included Christians who had

received infant baptism and those whose "alien immersion" was administered by non-Baptist communions.[6]

Landmarkism was a people's movement that in many ways mirrored the democratic idealism of the American experience. It was a powerful system for inculcating a peculiar Baptist identity, especially over against the development of another American religious community, the Campbell-Stone Restorationist Movement that produced three new denominations including the Disciples of Christ, the Christian Church, and the Churches of Christ. Restorationists claimed to have reconstituted the New Testament church, lost with the Constantinian/Roman church of the fourth century. Many Baptist churches and individuals moved into the "Christian Church." Landmarkists responded to the challenge by asserting that they needed no restoration since the Baptist lineage had remained intact since Jesus received John's baptism in the river Jordan. Landmark historiography remains an important source of identity for various Independent and Fundamentalist Baptist groups who associate Baptist successionism with biblical and theological orthodoxy.

Not all nineteenth-century Baptists accepted the Landmark view of history. One of the most significant challenges to Landmark hegemony in came from William Heth Whitsitt (1841–1911), president and professor of church history at the Southern Baptist Theological Seminary, Louisville, Kentucky. Using a seventeenth-century document known as the "Kiffin manuscript," Whitsitt concluded that Baptists had not practiced immersion when the General Baptists began in Amsterdam in 1608 or in London with the origins of the Particular Baptists in 1633. Rather, the practice originated around 1641, well after the movement was under way. This claim gave the lie to Landmark assertions that Baptists and Baptist-like sects had maintained immersions since Jesus' own baptism in the river Jordan. He wrote that "prior to 1641" both the General and Particular Baptists practiced sprinkling or pouring for baptism; in the year 1641 immersion was fetched out of Holland and a new epoch was introduced. There is no chance anywhere to evade that plain conclusion. If it may not stand secure, then the study of history is a delusion; no fact of history can ever be established.[7]

Whitsitt lamented the fact that earlier British Baptist historians had ignored these sources and perpetuated historical fallacies. He wrote that "with such ample collections as the British Museum, the Bodleian and other libraries lying just under their noses, it has seemed a sad hardship that in all these years they did not lift a finger to aid in the labor of investigating original sources."[8]

Whitsitt first released his discoveries in a congregational journal and in 1896 published *A Question in Baptist History*, a more extensive analysis of documents and details. Landmarkists were quick to respond, calling for his dismissal for having challenged the truth of Baptist doctrine and history. The seminary trustees refused to accept his resignation, but critics persisted and even pressed the SBC to cut off funds to the Louisville institution. Whitsitt resigned in 1898 and accepted a professorship at the University of Richmond. His research was later accepted by all but the most rabid Landmark supporters, and his methods forced Baptists to deal with the challenge of historical method over against popular, concocted historiography.

As a church historian, Whitsitt seemed to have understood the difficulties of revising popular history. In 1890 he wrote,

I am casting about to begin writing a work on American Baptist History. It is an Herculean task, and I must keep it all to myself. Baptist History is a department in which "the wise man concealeth knowledge." It is likely I shall not be able to publish the work while I live, but I can write it out in full and make arrangements to publish it after my death, when I shall be out of the reach of bigots and fools.[9]

His research was unacceptable because it contradicted the popular understanding of the uniqueness of Baptist identity as God's most biblical people.

Theological Diversity

Theories of origins have often made it difficult for Baptists to agree on a common historiography. Likewise, theological diversity impacted historical consciousness in fascinating ways. Intense theological debates, past and present, are informed by this historical reality: Baptists may be the only post-Reformation group that begins at both ends of the theological spectrum. The earliest Baptists in Amsterdam and England were General Baptists, Arminians who supported beliefs in prevenient grace, the general atonement, free will, and falling from grace. Close on their heels were the Particular Baptists, founded in London in the 1630s. Reformed Baptists supported election, predestination, limited atonement, and perseverance of the saints. Thus, from the beginning one could be a Calvinist or an Arminian all the while claiming the name Baptist. Calvinism prevailed as the dominant theological influence among the Regular Baptists who came to Charleston, South Carolina, in the 1690s and among the Separate Baptists who first showed up in North Carolina in the 1750s. Yet the "enthusiastical" preaching of the Separates opened the door to mass evangelism, which soon contributed to an implicit general atonement, greater emphasis on free will, and impetus for the mission movement.

In the South, certain groups—Primitive and Free Will Baptists—occupied either end of the theological spectrum, while others configured beliefs around modified Calvinism or Arminianism. Southern and Independent Baptists manifest what many call "moderate Calvinism" but which might as easily be designated a "moderate Arminianism." They used the language of Calvinism—election, predestination—but with a conversionism that tended toward Arminianism. Many were four-point Arminians and one-point Calvinists.

A Traditionless Tradition

In some respects, the Baptist communions referenced here reflect Sidney Mead's classic description of American Protestants as given to a "historylessness" whereby members justify their "peculiar interpretations and practices as more closely conforming to those of the early church as pictured in the New Testament than the views and policies of [their] rivals."[10] This traditionless tradition meant that some Baptists understood their history as simply a repetition of New Testament practices largely untouched by historical and theological influences present in the broader church or culture. In so doing, they sometimes viewed their particular belief and practice as untouched by the "traditions of men," those rites and regulations by which other Christian communions were bound. Others searched for that discernable identity formed in the earliest Baptist communities by which "real" Baptists could be identified in the present age. This fallacy of origins implied that there was one specific way of being Baptist and contemporary Baptists need only to find that way and model it. Would that it were that easy!

Tradition and Regional Identity

Baptist subgroups found identity and claimed a sense of historical consciousness around numerous issues in the church and the culture including a sense of southernness, denominationalism, doctrinal and ethical separatism, and Liberationist spirituality. Baptists in the South were indelibly shaped by southernness, an identity informed by their geographical location and its cultural heritage. From its beginnings in 1845, the SBC understood itself in terms related to its region, the defeat in the Civil War, and the development of what Charles Reagan Wilson has called "the religion of the Lost Cause."[11] As perhaps no other southern denomination, the SBC inculcated the great southern myth that the people who lost the war retained the vision. The defeated people would, even in defeat, be more moral, more orthodox, and more evangelistic than their northern counterparts could ever be.[12] That identity is exemplified in this statement from Alabama Baptist Levi Barton in 1946, a century after the denomination's founding:

> I am more tremendously convinced than ever that the last hope, the fairest hope, the only hope for evangelizing this world on New Testament principles is the Southern Baptist people represented in that Convention. I mean no unkindness to anybody on earth, but if you call that bigotry then make the most of it.[13]

Barton and other Southern Baptists understood themselves as having a particular biblical and historical mandate to evangelize the world. These southern Christians would carry out the church's evangelical calling as none had done before.

A later generation of Southern Baptist historians provided a fascinating method for attempting to contextualize the Convention's origins and public stands in support of slavery. The operative term was "sectionalism." In their histories of the SBC, W. W. Barnes and Robert Baker traced the origins of the SBC to cultural differences between North and South, southerners' complaints that they contributed the most money to the mission enterprise but they were "neglected in the appointment of missionaries,"[14] and the insults southerners endured from northern abolitionists. Slavery was thus listed in the context of numerous divisions between the two regions. Implicitly or explicitly, the sectionalism argument had the effect of minimizing or diluting the impact of slavery as the central issue in the founding of the SBC. In response, studies like John Lee Eighmy's *Churches in Cultural Captivity*, Rufus Spain's *At Ease in Zion*, and Samuel Hill's *Southern Churches in Crisis* explored the ways in which Southern Baptist triumphalism and regionalism combined to blind the constituency to social and racial deficiencies in their own environment.[15]

Members of the SBC were not the only ones impacted by southernness. Primitive and Old Regular Baptists understood themselves in terms of the "sacred space" of the southern mountains and the insular setting of their churches. As James Peacock and Ruel Tyson write, "'This country' is a phrase that these mountain Primitive Baptists use for the land that comprises their domain, more or less coterminous with the boundaries of their [Baptist] association."[16] It was in that region that the sovereign God had called them to preserve "old-timey" religion of a biblical people.

Southernness informed the historical consciousness of African Americans in ways both positive and negative. African American religious traditions took shape in the southern environment, in religious communities that had their own historical consciousness from slavery time to the exodus of blacks from white churches after the Civil War to the struggle for civil rights. At the same time, African American churches were compelled to assert a particular racial consciousness that set them against the proslavery or segregationist proof texts used by some white Baptists. This dichotomy of identities led Paul Harvey to challenge the thesis that the southern churches were simply in "cultural captivity." He wondered instead if there were points where "southern culture fell captive to southern religion." His study focuses on many types of Baptists in the South and southern cultures.[17] (Whatever else this may mean, it is clear that Baptists in the south understood themselves in terms of their region.)

More recently, Independent Baptists viewed southernness as delineating a fortress mentality of separation from the world. Regionally, the Bible Belt, most of it based in the South, was a last bastion in the fight against moral and spiritual decline. For many, a rejection of "worldliness" included mandates against drugs, alcohol, tobacco, pornography, rock and roll, movies (G-rated might be acceptable), and provocative dress on males and females. Divisions later occurred over the appropriateness of certain kinds of Christian music, moderation rather than abstinence in the use of alcohol, and the boundaries for Christian use of the media.

This regional and historical identity is undergoing transition at almost every level. Baptist groups, like others in the South, now confront the new southernness, a region whose traditional cultures are informed by or giving way to agendas set by pluralism, globalism, economics, and mass culture. Southern churches, even in the hollows of Appalachia, confront religious pluralism, not simply from innumerable Christian groups but from non-Christian religionists as well. There are Muslims, Buddhists, and Wiccans in Asheville, North Carolina, that Baptist-infested mountain town. Likewise, many persons now joining Baptist churches have little or no connection to traditional southernness beyond pop-culture caricatures of barbecue, NASCAR, and mountain hillbillies. In fact, the SBC has debated for years whether it should drop the word "southern" from its name since it was no longer simply a regional denomination. So far no change has been made.

Some Baptist churches in the South have worked hard to disassociate themselves from a solely regional identity. Still others, at least rhetorically, mourn the loss of certain values and family responses evident in southern culture among Caucasian and African Americans. These include issues related to divorce, same-sex unions, the drug culture, and women's role in church and family. In various ways all of the southern-based Baptist groups confront identity crises as they are forced to explore historical consciousness apart or distinct from southernness. In fact, many congregations are now at a transition period whereby older communicants struggle with how to move beyond the southernness that nurtured them and a newer generation who have less sense of that past and do not really want to be reminded of it.

The idea of a traditionless tradition has also been challenged by a younger group of scholars who reassert the need for Baptists "to acknowledge tradition in particular as a formal source of authority." As Baptist scholar Steven R. Harmon writes, "Tradition-retrieving Baptist theologians believe that becoming more conscious of the inescapable role of tradition in Christian faith and practice can help Baptists to distinguish between healthy and harmful sources of tradition."[18] Advocates of these views often refer to themselves as "Bapto-Catholics," concerned to connect to the apostolic roots of the early Christian centuries. They encourage Baptists to utilize historic creeds, not as extrabiblical mandates but as guides for linking Baptists with Christian orthodoxy past and present. Harmon believes that there is also

> potential . . . for a Baptist recovery of the authority of the communion sanctorum in an extension to the universal church (the existence of which is affirmed by mainstream Baptist ecclesiology, even if denied by 'Landmark' Baptists) of the Baptist ecclesiological principle that the local congregation as a community gathered under the Lordship of Christ possesses a certain derivative authority, subordinate to the Scriptures, for the ordering of its faith and practice.[19]

Tradition and Denominations

A second source of historical consciousness for Baptists is denominationalism, that organizational system that created a strong historical consciousness among those groups that accepted and rejected it. Southern Baptists continue to maintain one of the most elaborate denominational systems in the United States. The Southern Baptist denominational program provides members with an astounding sense of identity. Indeed, if members of the SBC have any sense of historical consciousness at all, it is grounded in their denominational identity. African American Baptists remain connected to specific denominations, although those connections seem to be a bit more fluid and overlapping than for members of the SBC. While less associated with a national or overarching denomination, mountain Baptists often claim historical consciousness as Primitive or Old Regular Baptists in particular relationship with their local or regional association of churches. They understand their denominational connections as a churchly link to historic associations.

Independent Baptists, while eschewing denominations and mission boards, often understand themselves historically in terms of their resistance to denominations, particularly the SBC.

Declining denominational consciousness, postdenominationalism, or whatever one calls the changing nature of American ecclesiastical organizations is fast descending on Baptist groups in the South. In the SBC, the twenty-year controversy between conservatives and moderates has been only one of the challenges to denominational identity. Moderates, now cut off from the SBC, are forced to define their own Baptistness apart from the denominational identity that nurtured them. Often the loss of denominational connections forces churches to decide what it means to be Baptist beyond the denominational context. Conservatives in the new SBC are not without problems, however, in passing on denominational identity to a new generation hesitant to claim denominational labels too quickly. Appalachian Baptists also find it difficult to pass on historical consciousness given the impact of religious television and the mobility of a new generation of young people, many of whom move to town or out of the region entirely. Independent Baptists, long antagonistic to denominationalism, now find that some of their churches have affiliated with the SBC, welcomed back to a denomination that now mirrors their own theological fundamentalism. Southern Independent and African American Baptist churches are now relinquishing or minimizing the Baptist name in an effort to attract seekers "turned off" by "brand-name religion." African American churches, long connected to various national Baptist conventions, are also experiencing transitions as the megachurch model becomes increasingly prominent as evident in the work of Bishop Eddie Long, Reverend Creflo Dollar, and Bishop T. D. Jakes.

Perhaps there is no greater challenge to denominational identity than the so-called megachurch movement. Megachurches are congregations of several thousand members, led by a charismatic, CEO, authority-figure pastor, providing specialized ministries to

target groups and organized around intentional marketing techniques. Megachurches are often self-defined as "seeker-oriented"
churches primarily aimed at persons who are religiously nonaffili-
ated. Their worship is often more contemporary, with praise choruses projected on screens around the "worship centers," replacing
traditional hymns. Services are informal in liturgy and dress, often
including dramas or skits. Megachurches may eschew or relinquish denominational "brand" names, in favor of the designation
"community church" or "fellowship." In a sense, megachurches are
minidenominations, offering in one congregation services, ministries, and connections that were formerly offered to multiple
churches by regional and national denominations. While some of
these churches are connected to national denominations, many are
free-standing congregations that emphasize their nondenominational nature. Baptist groups in the South are affected by the megachurch movement and its influence on issues of worship, polity,
and identity.

Churches that appropriate megachurch influences may encounter renewed vigor in their services as well as divisions over changes
in worship traditions. While popular and highly successful, megachurches have yet to show that they can pass on a tradition or identity to a second generation of believer/consumers. Indeed, given
the tendency of megachurches to maintain a looser, more generic
form of Christianity, it remains to be seen what kind of identity
might be passed on.

Tradition and Baptist Separatism

A third category of historical consciousness among these Baptist
groups included separatism, an idea that Christian and Baptist
commitments required separation from the world, offering a dog-
matic or moralistic front against the onslaughts of worldliness and
secular corruption. Separation from the world involved many outward evidences. Baptists throughout America carried out public
disciplining of members well into the twentieth century. Among

Appalachian Baptists it was not uncommon for morally recalcitrant members to be "churched," excommunicated from the congregation and shunned by the faithful. Twentieth-century African
American Baptist churches often faced an imposed separatism in a
segregated, Jim Crow society. This led to the development of identities informed by that reality in which church was a major factor
in family, community, and racial life. While some of that loyalty
remains intact, there are signs that it is cracking with the opening
of other opportunities in the broader society.

Independent Baptists have actually been known as Baptist separatists due to their belief that all contact with liberals is a compromise of the faith. Their assertion is this: "to know a liberal is to be
a liberal." Any direct or indirect connection with liberalism would
lead to doctrinal compromise. Orthodoxy of belief and practice
meant separation from the world and an uncompromising ethic as
set forth by the church. This separatism led many Independent Baptists to dismiss Billy Graham when the famous evangelist invited
Methodists, Presbyterians, and other "liberals" to participate in his
crusades. When Catholics were included the break was complete.
Separatism was one reason that many Independent Baptists kept
out of politics or political involvement.

As Independent Baptists have chosen to participate in the New
Political Religious Right, they have found their separatism challenged. This was evident in Jerry Falwell's decision to include Mor-
mons and Catholics in the membership of the Moral Majority, a
dramatic change in older separatist ideology and practice.

Likewise, Baptist groups have experienced major identity crises regarding the moral separatism that long characterized their
communions. New definitions of "worldliness" have divided Baptist groups across the theological landscape. Gambling, the use of
alcohol and tobacco, dress codes, sexual mores, materialism, and
other issues have all been challenged. In some respects many of
the Baptists still claim moral separatism from the world. Leaders of these groups, black and white, appear on national media to

speak as counterculture voices challenging the prevailing ethical or unethical values inside the culture. Attacks on the "homosexual agenda" suggest that it is destructive to American family and social life. Secularization is viewed as a new religious establishment to be opposed by Baptist dissenters who feel their liberties undermined by state sanction of secular agendas. Yet a closer look reveals other segments of the culture—materialism, media, and establishmentarianism—that suggest a compromise with at least certain parts of the world. Richard Quebedeaux called such Christians the "worldly evangelicals."[20]

Tradition and Conversionism

With a strong emphasis on a believers' church, Baptists cultivated a historical consciousness closely connected to evangelical conversionism and the call for a direct, transforming experience of divine grace. While a regenerate church membership was a formative element of Baptist ecclesiology from the beginning of the movement, periods of religious awakening in Britain and America made revivalism a morphology or process that shaped the way individuals and churches understood the nature and purpose of conversion. Revivals were a common form of evangelical and spiritual renewal for Independent, African American, and Southern Baptists. Only Primitive and Old Regular Baptists rejected them as a garish form of works righteousness outside the salvific boundaries set by the sovereign God.

Of the southern form of this evangelicalism, Paul Harvey writes,

> Evangelical Protestantism ordered the lives of millions of common folk in the South long after its central role in other parts of the country had been diminished. The southern evangelical emphasis on direct, immediate and vibrantly emotional contact with God has given the South its distinctive religious coloration.[21]

For frontier and rural congregations, revival meetings were held seasonally, often in spring after planting and in fall after harvest. Preaching was usually carried out by a visiting evangelist/preacher during meetings which lasted two weeks or more. Often these were community events, drawing large crowds from many Christian traditions. Revivals were characterized by lively music, "personal testimonies" from the converted, colorful sermons by the evangelist, and the urging of sinners to repentance. Church members were encouraged to bring the unconverted to the services, sometimes through friendly competition in "pack the pew nights," in which prizes were given to those who brought the most people. Conversion brought life-changing spirituality by which one turned from "death to life," turned toward Christian discipleship, and, in some cases, sought to transform society individually or collectively.

Baptists in the South, black and white, created an extensive revivalist culture that shaped the methods and theology for accomplishing evangelism. While they were particularly significant in rural areas and small towns, revivals were also brought to the city with "crusades" held in urban stadiums and convention centers. Billy Graham was not the only Baptist evangelist to fill stadiums across the South during the second half of the twentieth century. With time, and the distractions of modern life, however, many churches shortened revival meetings to a week, then to Sunday to Wednesday. The revival culture became less appealing to many urbanites inside and outside the churches. Revival methods, established in an earlier, more rural, less secular era, were increasingly difficult to sustain. By the later twentieth century, while some churches continued to conduct revivals, many had dropped them from the church calendar, substituting spiritual renewal services or other occasions not characterized by revival formats. Revivals continue to be utilized in some Baptist churches in the region, black and white. In those congregations they still inform a sense of historical consciousness linking the churches with their evangelical past, providing important and tangible means of converting sinners. In other churches, the loss or decline of those specific methods raises questions about what to offer in their place.

Revivalistic zeal was the means by which these Baptists would convert the region and the world. Use of revival methodology did not mean, however, that Baptists shared a common historical consciousness as to the meaning and ultimate implications of conversion. Conversionistic imperatives pushed many Anglo-Saxon Baptists to stress the importance of individual salvation and moralism while often hesitating to press for changes in the society, especially in its segregationist traditions. Richard Furman's 1822 defense of slavery found sanction in the New Testament church for slavery as a social given, even as he urged the conversion of slaves. African Americans, however, linked spiritual liberation with social and racial liberation. They often found in their deliverance from sin a negation of slavery. The connection between conversionism for individual and society was an important historical consciousness for those African Americans who fought the separate but equal system of the American South.

A variety of social and theological transitions has challenged Baptists' understanding of the nature and importance of conversionism and Liberationist ideals. The decline of revivalism as a method has caused some churches to have to revisit their theology of evangelism and conversion. How does conversion occur outside a revivalistic context? What is the relationship of conversion to the role of women in the church? Does conversion free all persons to respond to a call to ministry regardless of their gender? Can Liberationist and Conversionist ideals be applied to the liberation of gays and lesbians inside the church?

Baptist piety also sent women to seminaries. Youth camps, Sunday schools, and revival services impressed upon Baptist youth the need to "do whatever God calls you to do." Indeed, Southern Baptist young people grew up singing such hymns as "Wherever He Leads, I'll Go" and "I Surrender All." When females took those admonitions to their logical conclusions and moved toward all facets of Christian ministry (including pastorates), some Baptists protested. Divisions over the role of women in ministry paralleled, even contradicted, some of the pious generalizations about the boundaries of Christian service.

While an emphasis on evangelism continues and concerns for baptisms and church growth remain strong, the decreasing use of revival methodology has created questions as to what new models for doing evangelism might be developed.

This transition in Conversionist identity leads some to suggest that Baptists are best defined by what they must believe. Some Confessionalists even propose using one specific theological tradition—Calvinism—to inform their reading of the denomination's confession of faith and other doctrinal statements.

Others insist the Baptist essence is found not in "man-made" creeds but in being a "free and faithful" people, bound to Scripture, community, and individual conscience. Still others are concerned to understand the Baptist heritage in light of the broader mainline, evangelical, or even charismatic movements in the church at large. Some, however, seem to act as if the old mechanisms are still intact, relying on the denominational system to inform identity.

Fundamentalists insist that theirs is the true Baptist vision because they, like early Baptists, are committed to the infallible and inerrant Word of God. Moderates declare that they possess the identity passed on from "free and faithful" Baptists to a new generation of believers. Women wonder if they can ever get beyond the "woman's sphere" or the ecclesiastical "glass ceiling" to claim full identity among the people who nurtured them to faith and ministry. Many others question the continuing divisions between Baptists, black and white, in America.

Renewing Baptist Identity

In light of this diversity in Baptist self-definition, what strategies might Baptists use in recovering, renewing, or restating their identity?

First, local congregations must exercise greater intentionality in exploring and defining the nature of the Baptist heritage for themselves. In an earlier time, the denomination was the chief resource for identity, communicated through literature, educational programs, missionary outreach, and the general ethos of a rather homogenous American culture. Toward the future local congregations must be intentional about the need for identity, given the diversity of Baptist stories and traditions, the specific traditions they seek to communicate, preserve, and promote.

Second, Baptists should not succumb to the fallacy of origins, that noble but naive belief that there exists a pristine, systematic, and unified source of Baptist identity in the beginning that need only be discovered and installed. In fact, there are multiple Baptist traditions—theological, regional, and institutional—from which churches may choose. There are many Baptist "stories" from which congregations and individuals may draw, some complimentary, others contradictory. Discovering the story or stories that most inform what kind of Baptist one person or community of faith wishes to be is one of the great adventures for Baptist people toward the new century.

Third, Baptists might come to understand their classic "distinctives" as significant ideals that are ever held in tension, in a continuing and elusive quest for balance. For example, like their forebearers, Baptist communions might seek to maintain a robust biblicism informed by an equally robust concern for "soul liberty," the freedom of individual and communal interpretation. A concern for a church of believers might lead them to bring persons to conversion through means of both gentle nurture and dramatic religious experience. Baptist churches could reexamine the meaning of believers' baptism and the Lord's Supper and the role of these sacraments (ordinances), not simply within the congregation but within the entire church of Jesus Christ. Given the transitions, even breakdowns, in old denominational connections, Baptists in the South must reconsider the relationship between local autonomy and associational or ecumenical cooperation. Likewise, the concern for the priesthood of all believers should not lead to the idea that being a Baptist means that one can believe anything at all. Rather, the individual "priest" exists within and is informed by the community of "priests," the church.

Fourth, Baptists would do well to continue to cultivate their role as religious dissenters from establishments political and religious. Clearly, Baptists themselves will not agree on when and where dissent is necessary, but they should struggle with it nonetheless. Whether fighting for religious liberty in Virginia or civil rights in Alabama, Baptists in the South (black and white) have upheld a proud tradition of dissent. Toward the future, they might pursue the essence of religious dissent and the wisdom to know when to exercise it.

Finally, Baptists might remember that historically and theologically there are many ways to be a Baptist. There are many stories, some contradictory, that inform Baptist identity. In the future, Baptists are called upon to choose which story or stories best inform who they are and wish to be under God. They might also think long and hard before relinquishing the name Baptist in favor of some nebulous, generic religious ethos. Religion has specificity and offers a place to stand from which to relate to other movements and ideas in the religious marketplace of global pluralism.

3

BAPTIST POLITY
A People's Church
❋

In a confession of faith written in 1611 and titled A Declaration of Faith of English People Remaining at Amsterdam in Holland, the earliest Baptists described the congregational polity of their new communion. The article declared,

> That as one congregation hath CHRIST, so hath all, 2. Cor. 10.7. And that the Word Of GOD cometh not out from any one, neither to any one congregation in particular. I. Cor. 14.36. But unto every particular Church, as it doth unto all the world. Coll. 1.5.6. And therefore no church ought to challenge any prerogative over any other.[1]

Baptists began, and to a great extent continue, as a Christian communion grounded in a radical congregational polity. They are ever struggling with the tension between individual autonomy and corporate connectionalism. Baptists are indeed a people's movement, at the center of the so-called Free Church Tradition. Baptist congregations move across a spectrum that runs from rabid localism and individualism to varying degrees of communal and denominational conformity. The Baptist system of ecclesiastical order creates a dramatic sense of freedom for individuals and churches to determine

39

their own directions in Christ, but such populism ensures dissent, disagreement, and the potential for schism at every turn.

Baptists began with a radical congregationalism and the idea that Christ's authority was mediated not through bishop or king but through the congregation of Christian believers. The congregation bore the authority for administering the sacraments, preaching, ordaining, and determining the nature of its own ministry. Yet no sooner was the movement under way than individual congregations created "associations" with other like-minded churches for fellowship, mutual encouragement, doctrinal solidarity, and other connectional interactions. Early associations in Britain and America developed extensive influence, exercising varying degrees of authority among cooperating churches. Associational cooperation was important because it linked fledgling churches for fellowship, offered a resource for advice in doctrinal disputes, and (if invited) could serve as a mediator in church conflicts. The association created a sense of the larger community of like-hearted churches beyond the local congregation.

Yet an uneasy tension often existed between local congregations and corporate associations, particularly when local autonomy was threatened by authoritarian bureaucracies. To this day, Baptist polity retains an elusive quality. Writing in the twentieth century (1947) Henry Cook observed, "Strictly speaking there is no such thing as 'Baptist polity,' because Baptists by their own fundamental principle are committed to accepting the Church polity of the New Testament, and no-one can really say with positive certainty what that actually is."[2] In other words, the question for Congregationalists is less *what* is the polity of the New Testament than *which* New Testament polity shall become normative.

Amid associational and denominational connections, local autonomy, individual freedom, and congregational church government combined to make schism, debate, and division an everpresent reality in Baptist life. In her study of American frontier religion, Christine Leigh Heyrman described the tendency of Baptist churches to split over a variety of issues and suggested that "the absence of any authoritative higher body left the Baptists with no means of settling disputes among the clergy, generational or otherwise." Heyrman thus concluded that when conflicts arose, "the Baptists could only wait and hope for a resolution after the bloodletting over contested leadership engulfed and then exhausted their churches. Given their abiding devotion to congregational independence, a veritable icon of lay adoration, the Baptists could not have handled matters differently and still remained Baptists."[3] Congregational polity and its application in Baptist churches often mean that debates and divisions are not only possible, they are probable. The old saying that Baptists "multiply by dividing" is in large part an inevitable result of their polity.

Baptist Beginnings

The first Baptists appeared in Holland as early as 1608–1609 among a group of English Separatist Puritans exiled from their homeland amid the persecution of dissenters by the new Stuart monarchy. In Amsterdam they had contact with the "Ancient Church" founded by Francis Johnson, its name derived from the congregation's desire to emulate the faith and practice of the New Testament community. They were not unaffected by the writings of Separatist leader Robert Browne (1550?–1633) as delineated in his work *A Treatise for Reformation without Tarying for Anie* (1580). In it he asserted that the church was a congregation of believers bound to Christ and each other by a covenantal relationship. British historian B. R. White proposed that the early Baptists "inherited" many of their views from the Separatists, particularly the idea of covenant as the foundational principle for the founding of a church and the belief that the congregational appointment of leaders was "proscribed in [God's] Word." Congregational authority empowered the community of faith to exercise discipline and act under Christ's authority.[4]

John Smyth (1570?–1612?), the spiritual leader of the group, was joined in his efforts by Thomas Helwys (1550?–1616?), a member of England's "lesser gentry" who helped finance the journey of the exiles to Amsterdam. The two came to the conclusion that the true church was composed of believers only, those who could testify to an experience of divine grace and own the covenant with God and their fellow Christians. Baptism, therefore, was to be administered only after faith was professed, an act that was impossible to infants. Thus, probably in 1609, Smyth, Helwys, and the little band of Separatists repudiated their earlier infant baptism, confessed faith in Christ, received a new baptism, and constituted a church, history's first Baptist communion. To begin this new believers' church, Smyth baptized himself and then baptized the others, probably by trine affusion, pouring water on the head three times in the name of the Father, the Son, and the Holy Spirit. The polity of the church was clearly congregational.

The early confession cited earlier defined the church of Christ as "a company of faithful people I Cor. 1, 2. Eph. 1.1. separated from the world by the word & Spirit of GOD. 2 Cor, 6, 17. being knit unto the LORD, & one unto another, by Baptism. I Cor. 12.13. Upon their own confession of the faith. Act. 8.37. and sins. Mat. 3.6." Members were received by baptism "upon confession of their faith and sins. . . . And therefore Churches constituted after any other manner, or of any other persons are not according to CHRIST'S testament."[5]

General Baptist is the term we use to describe the group in Amsterdam due to their affirmation of prevenient grace, free will, falling from grace, and the general atonement of Jesus Christ. As they saw it, all persons were potentially elected to salvation and actually elected if they came on the terms of election, repentance, and faith. John Smyth remained with the Amsterdam group for a short time until he became convinced that the Mennonites in Amsterdam had a more legitimate baptismal tradition. He repudiated his self-baptism and, with others of the Baptists, petitioned the

Mennonites for membership. He died waiting on their decision. Helwys took the remaining group and returned to England around 1612 where they founded a church near Spitalfields, outside the London wall.

By the 1630s a second group of Baptists had appeared in London, these growing directly out of the Non-Conformist, Independent Movement of English Puritanism, specifically out of the so-called Jacob-Lathrop-Jessey Church. This group also affirmed congregational polity but in the context of Reformed theology. They are known as Particular Baptists because of their affirmation of Christ's limited or particular atonement, efficacious only for the elect chosen before the foundation of the world.

Though occupying either end of the theological spectrum in matters of election, predestination, and free will, these Baptist groups agreed on matters of church government, church officers, and congregational life. The seventeenth-century confessions of faith from both General and Particular Baptists illustrate their common approaches to polity. They seem to have constituted themselves around a covenant "or solemn agreement with God and with one another."[6] Oxford theologian Paul S. Fiddes suggests that for these Baptists covenants had four applications. First, there was "God's covenant of grace" made "with human beings and angels for their salvation in Jesus Christ." Second, there was covenant as a transaction in the Godhead in which the Son consented "to the will of the Father to undertake the work of the salvation of the elect." Third, God made an agreement "corporately" with the entire church and with specific congregations. Fourth, covenant was an agreement binding believers to a specific church and to each other.[7] Baptist historian Karen Smith suggests that covenants gave attention to the church as "a visible community of saints" whose members pledged to join together in "worship, prayer for one another, attendance for the ordinances, and participation in the discipline and government of the congregation."[8]

Covenants and polity began with the believers' church. Only those who could profess faith in Christ and receive believers' baptism were appropriate members of the church and participants in the covenant of grace. The London Confession of 1644 declared, "To this Church he [Christ] hath made his promises, and given the signs of his Covenant, presence, love, blessing, and protection: here are the fountains and springs of his heavenly grace continually flowing forth." All believers were "fitly compact and knit together, according to the effectual working of every part, to the edification of itself in love."[9]

Covenant also meant that the authority of Christ was given to the entire congregation and mediated through the community of believers. This is clear in the way the London Confession of 1644 described the nature of discipline and its place in the church. It states that "Christ has likewise given power to his whole Church to receive in and cast out, by way of Excommunication, any member; and this power is given to every particular Congregation, and not one particular person, either member or Officer, but the whole."[10] Christ's authority came to the church not through bishops, presbyteries, or judicatories but through the congregation itself. Members worked by consensus if possible, majority rule if not.

Early congregational polity meant a close relationship between individual and corporate faith. In many Baptist churches in Britain and North America, converts were required to relate details of their conversion to the congregation or its elders who then determined if it was indeed a valid experience. Sometimes the sinner was required to "try again" or "wait on the Lord" before baptism and church membership were permitted. Discipline was a real possibility, and church records are filled with accounts of disciplinary action meted out by congregations against recalcitrant members.

Church Officers

This congregational polity posited two officers, set aside by the laying on of hands. These included pastors or elders who shared in the ministry of the word and deacons who were responsible for responding to the physical needs of the faithful. The Amsterdam Confession (1611) stated clearly and concisely, "That the Officers of every Church or congregation are either Elders, who by their office do especially feed the flock concerning their souls, Act. 20.28, Pet. 5.2, 3. or Deacons Men and Women who by their office relieve the necessities of the poor and impotent brethren concerning their bodies, Acts. 6.1-4."[11] That early statement generally reflects the nature of Baptist ministry into the twenty-first century.

By the mid-1650s some of these Baptists had defined their belief and practice in terms of the "Six Principles" set forth in Hebrews 6:1-2. It reads, "Therefore let us go on toward perfection, leaving behind the basic teaching about Christ, and not laying again the foundation; repentance from dead works and faith toward God, instruction about baptisms, laying on of hands, resurrection of the dead, and eternal judgment." In affirming these six doctrines as a basic description of Baptist identity, these "Six Principle Baptists" also practiced the laying on of hands in two installments. The first, administered to all who received baptism, was a sign that all believers had received the Holy Spirit and in a sense were ministers, called to labor together with God in the world. The second observance of the laying on of hands was given to those set aside for peculiar ministry in the church. In this the Baptists paralleled the Quakers by recognizing that all the faithful had a calling to ministry by virtue of faith in Christ; yet they went beyond the Quakers in retaining an ordained clergy who shared especially in the ministry of the word within the believing community.[12] Both Particular and General Baptists appropriated the "Six Principles" into their congregations.

This concern for ministry among both clergy and laity led to differences in congregational approach to the administration of the sacraments. Some Baptist churches permitted any individual duly elected by the congregation, ordained or not, to serve at baptism or the Lord's Supper. Others explicitly required only ordained persons to preside at those events. In 1693 the Western Assembly of British Baptists determined that "no private brother (however gifted) if not solemnly called to ministerial office and separated thereto ought to administer the ordinance of baptism or the Last Supper."[13]

Baptist Associations

Baptists were deeply committed to the autonomy of the congregation but also developed associational relationships with other congregations. They were surprisingly quick to reach out to other Baptists. The London Confession (1644) described those relationships accordingly:

> And although the particular Congregations be distinct and several Bodies, every one a compact and knit City in itself; yet are they all to walk by one and the same Rule, and by all means convenient to have the counsel and help one of another in all needful affairs of the Church, as members of one body in the common faith under Christ their only head.[14]

Baptist associations are gatherings of churches usually in a given geographic region, linked for fellowship, mutual encouragement, and extended ministries. Associations represent one of the earliest forms of Baptist connectionalism and "denominational" organization. Baptist historian W. T. Whitley wrote that "Baptists from the beginning sought to maintain sisterly intercourse between local churches; they never thought that one church was independent of others."[15]

Yet even the associational relationships were not permitted to undermine or threaten the uniqueness of the local church. The Second London Confession of 1677 (Particular Baptist) acknowledged that "in cases of difficulties or differences" related to one or multiple congregations "it is according to the mind of Christ, that many Churches holding communion together, do by their messengers meet to consider, and give their advice in, or about that matter in difference, to be reported to all the Churches concerned." Yet while they might give advice, the messengers were "not entrusted with any Church-power properly so called; or with any jurisdiction over the Churches themselves, to exercise any censures either over any Churches, or Persons; or to impose their determination on the Churches or officers."[16]. Baptists tend to struggle with the relationship between clergy and laity, between the priesthood of the laity and the leadership of an ordained ministry. Congregationalism means that power often moves back and forth between the ordained and lay leaders.

Baptist Polity: Developing Options

Strangely, many of the seventeenth-century approaches to Baptist polity describe existing Baptist congregational structures. Congregational authority tends to be the basis for Baptist church life. Congregations may relate to local associations, state Baptist conventions, and national denominations, but ideally those broader organizations defer when necessary to the local church. Some Baptists even eschew denominations altogether lest they undermine the basis of Baptist localism. Many expressed mistrust of any alliances that promoted "hierarchies" outside the local church.

Denominationalism has developed in many Baptist communions, however. Several of the earliest regional or national Baptist connections began in response to the modern missions movement when they pooled resources in order to fund ministry and evangelism abroad. The Baptist Missionary Society, founded in London in 1792, was supported by churches throughout England to provide funds for the missionary enterprise. In America, the General Convention of the Baptist Denomination in the United States for Foreign Missions (Triennial Convention) was founded in 1814 when three congregational missionaries on their way to India converted to Baptist views and asked for support. Since single congregations did not have the funds to carry out such programs, they were required to pool their resources to support missions. These efforts reflected a denominationalizing influence, but even then many Baptists were fearful that a "hierarchy" would result that would threaten the autonomy of congregations.

To protect autonomy, these Baptists formed individual societies with special tasks for supporting home and foreign missions, publications, evangelism, and education. Each society was itself autonomous, maintaining its own independent board of directors and raising its own funds for its special endeavors. Membership in the societies was extended to individuals, churches, or associations who contributed funds to support of the specific project.

Francis Wayland (1796–1865), an American Baptist pastor and longtime president of Brown University, was an early supporter of denominational connectionalism. In the 1820s he proposed that "the model of our system of general and state government will at once suggest itself to every American. The Associations in one state could easily send delegates to a state convention. This would embody all the information, and concentrate energies of a state. These state conventions might be brought to concentrated and united action." Wayland was clear that such affiliations would not include "any creeds or articles to be imposed on ourselves, or our brethren. The Bible is our only standard, and it is a sufficient standard of faith and practice."[17] He later repudiated those views, concerned that the denominational mechanisms had indeed threatened the authority of the congregation. He renewed emphasis on the society method as a way of accomplishing ministry without creating hierarchy. Wayland wrote, "A missionary society is not a representative body, nor can any number of them speak the language of a whole denomination." The members of each society joined together "not as representatives of churches, for the churches have never sent them nor commissioned them; they come together on their own motion, merely as members of the Union, or of the Home Mission, or Bible, or any other society."[18] The dilemma of relationships between denominations and local churches haunts Baptist polity to this day.

Nineteenth-century Landmarkists challenged denominational structures by insisting that the sole basis of Baptist polity was the local congregation since from their perspective the Greek word *ecclesia* referred only to a local expression of the church. Mission boards and other denominational programs threatened the authority of the local church and should be ignored or severely limited in their authority. The Landmark influence is reflected in the disdain for denominations evident among Independent Baptists in the United States.

Contemporary Baptists

In one sense twenty-first-century Baptists share a common polity with their seventeenth-century forebearers. Most continue to affirm the centrality of the local church, join in associational relationships, and, with some exceptions, form conventions, societies, or unions with like-minded Baptists in their regions or nations. For example, the breakup of the Soviet Union produced numerous new Baptist unions in countries such as Romania, Latvia, Georgia, Poland, and Lithuania. Generally speaking, these unions or denominations are derivative in authority from local churches. Individual congregations elect their own officers, search for and select their own ministers, raise their own budgets, and pursue their own specific ministries. Governance is generally expressed by majority vote with various lay committees charged with carrying out specific aspects of church life and governance.

Of the roughly forty million Baptists in the world, over thirty million are in the United States, where there are at least fifty distinct groups of Baptist denominations or fellowships. Their theologies cover the spectrum from free will Arminians to Predestinarian Calvinists, with multiple movements in between. All of these groups practice varying forms of congregational polity in autonomous congregations that ordain ministers, define ministries, relate to regional, state, and national bodies (or not), and fund their own budgets. Currently, debates over the ordination of women, ministerial authority, biblical inerrancy, homosexuality, abortion, baptism, denominational participation, and other controversial issues divide individuals, churches, and denominations themselves. Congregational polity means all members have voice (potentially) in church affairs and that congregations can determine their own futures based on consensus of the community. This polity means that individual churches can make choices on either side of controversial issues without *necessarily* dividing the entire denomination. For example, one Baptist church may choose to ordain women while another chooses not to do so, yet they remain in the same Baptist denomination. (This possibility is increasingly difficult to sustain.) However, problems arise. These include,

1. The absence of effective moderators for church disputes
2. The dynamics of clergy/laity power blocs in congregations
3. The difficulties of placement and personal trauma faced by ministers who have been terminated by one congregation
4. Continued divisions and polarization that make collective ministry increasingly difficult
5. A growing emphasis on individualism in the church and in the society that undermines community in Baptist life

These are but a few of the issues that are increasing the questions of identity among Baptists in the United States and around the world.

Walter Rauschenbusch (1861–1918), Baptist pastor and professor and father of the Social Gospel Movement, wrote of this polity,

> Our churches are Christian democracies. The people are sovereign in them. All power wielded by the church's ministers and

officers is conferred by the church. It makes ample room for those who have God-given powers for leadership, but it holds them down to the service of the people by making them responsible to the church for their actions. That democracy of the Baptist church is something to be proud of.[19]

This rather idyllic description of Baptist church government belies the difficulties of this democratic method. From the beginning of the movement Baptists have been plagued by schisms, divisions, and intra- and interchurch feuds that have led to new churches, associations, and groups. If each church is free to set its own directions and ministries, then associations and denominations are also free to dismiss those whose ideas and positions differ. While the will of the majority prevails, dissent by individuals or minorities is an ever-present reality. Being Baptist is messy, controversial, and divisive. Like the gospel.

Hmm...

4

BIBLICIST BUT NOT BIBLE?

Revisiting Baptist Hermeneutics

In 1608 Baptist founder John Smyth wrote to distinguish his constantly changing theology from that of the "brethren of the separation," those Puritans with whom he had departed from the Church of England, a church he called "anti-Christ." While his views on church government and Scripture differed significantly from the Presbyterian-Separatists with whom he was previously aligned, Smyth nonetheless agreed with them as to the foundation of the "true church" as distinguished from the "falsehood" of the Anglicans. He wrote,

> Herein therefore especially are those auncient brethren to be honoured, that they have reduced the Church to the true Primitive & Apostolique constitution which consisteth in these three things. 1. The true matter which are sayntes only. 2. The true forme which is the uniting of them together in the covenant. 3. The true propertie which is communion in all holy things, & the power of the L. Iesus Christ, for the maintaining of that communion.[1]

Some four hundred years later, John Smyth—Anglican, Puritan, Separatist, founding Baptist, and would-be Mennonite—offers insight into the way the early Baptists understood themselves as a believers' church, a covenant people, and a true Church of Christ. Smyth's short statement, addressed to "the brethren of the separation," from whence he came, summarized ideas essential to Baptist identity then and now—the church as centered in the "true Primitive & Apostolique constitution" (biblicism), the church as a community of "sayntes" (conversionism), and the church as a covenant community held together by the "power of the L. Iesus Christ" (congregational sacramentalism). Those ideas offer an opportunity for revisiting Baptist identity in terms of biblicism, conversionism, and what might be called congregational sacramentalism. They also suggest ways for reflecting on the future of Baptist identity in the twenty-first century, a so-called postmodern moment when the future of the Baptists worldwide is unclear and their cultural dominance in the United States is coming to an end.

The Bible and Baptist Confessions of Faith

When it comes to defining the nature of Baptist identity, the confessions of faith are surprisingly uniform. In fact, whether written by General, Particular or Seventh Day, Six Principle, or Two-Seed-in-the-Spirit-Predestinarian Baptists, the confessions of faith reflect an uncanny consensus as to the nature of certain common Baptist ideals. They affirm

- The authority of Scripture and the freedom of conscience in matters of religion
- The church as a community of believers who can testify to an experience of grace through Jesus Christ
- Two sacraments/ordinances of baptism and the Lord's Supper (some later include the washing of feet as a biblical mandate)
- Baptism by immersion as a normative act for believers only (that mode became normative some thirty years after the movement began)

- The autonomy of the local congregation and the fellowship of congregations in "associational" relationships
- The priesthood of all believers and the ordaining of clergy
- Freedom of religion amid a loyalty to the state.

That Baptist people the world over continue to reflect significant commitment to those distinctives is truly remarkable given the breadth of Baptist theological and cultural diversity.

From their beginnings in seventeenth-century Holland and England, Baptists made it clear that the Bible was the primary source of inspiration and authority for congregations and individual believers. Born of English Separatist Puritanism with rudimentary kinship to the Radical Reformation, the earliest Baptist communions wrote confessions of faith that delineated basic beliefs as supported by Holy Scripture. Although they were second-generation Protestants, founded at least a century after the Reformation began, they unashamedly affirmed the Reformers' idea of *sola scriptura*, that Scripture alone is normative for the life and faith of the believing community. As second-generation Protestants, they carried the corresponding Reformation ideas of *sola fide* and *sola gratia* (faith alone and grace alone) a step further than most of their Protestant forebearers by requiring conversion of all who would claim church membership—a relatively new mandate in Christian history. Then they went beyond their Puritan colleagues by rejecting establishmentarian Protestantism and renouncing infant baptism in favor of the immersion of adult believers. Their simple biblicism challenged the prevailing link between infant baptism and European citizenship, a radical act of both heresy and treason.

Thus Baptist biblicism made a commitment to the authority of Scripture normative for faith and practice, while Baptist conversionism (spirituality) offered a powerful option for modifying that biblicism in the face of theological or cultural contradictions. At certain times Baptists asserted that the text of Scripture was a nonnegotiable element of their response to issues in the church and the culture. At other times they appealed to conversionism and pietistic spirituality when biblical literalism became ecclesiastically or culturally problematic.

Such biblicism was there from the beginning. In a 1691 treatise addressed to "all the Baptized Congregations in England and Wales," Baptist pastor Benjamin Keach noted his great joy when he considered

> the exceeding Grace and abounding Goodness of the Holy God towards you his poor and despised Church and People, in respect of that clear Discovery he hath given you of most of the glorious Truths of the Gospel, and of the true Apostolical Faith and Practice thereof. You have not made Men, General Councils, nor synods, your Rule, but God's Holy Word: your constitution.[2]

Like John Smyth before him, Keach insisted that Baptist identity was grounded in "Apostolical Faith and Practice," based in "God's Holy Word," not in the edicts of church councils, synods, or the doctrines of "Men."

Many seventeenth-century confessions of faith echo Keach's biblicism. The Declaration of Faith of English People (1611), written by the earliest General Baptists in Amsterdam, states,

> That the books of the Old and New Testament are written for our instruction, 2. Tim. 3.16 & that we ought to search them for they testifie of CHRIST, Jo. 5.39. And therefore to be used withal reverence, as conteyning the Holie Word of GOD, which only is our direction in al thinges whatsoever.[3]

In 1644, the London Confession of Particular (Calvinist) Baptists asserted that

> The Rule of this Knowledge, Faith, and Obedience . . . is not mans inventions, opinions, devices, lawes, constitutions, or traditions unwritten whatsoever, but only the word of God con-

tained in the Canonicall Scriptures. In this written Word God
hath plainly revealed whatsoever he hath thought needful for us
to know, believe, and acknowledge.[4]

The Orthodox Creed, published in 1679, one of the most fascinating if anomalous of the Baptist confessions, was an effort to
bring Arminian and Calvinist Baptists into closer agreement on the
essential dogmas. The statement on Scripture affirms that biblical
truth does not rest on the "authority of any man, but only upon
the authority of God." In a critique directed at Quakers and other
Charismatics, the confession cautions, "Neither ought we, since we
have the scriptures delivered to us now, to depend upon, hearken
to, or regard the pretended immediate inspiration, dreams, or pro-
phetical predictions by or from any person whatsoever, lest we be
deluded by them."[5] In a singular rejection of Catholic claims regarding the unity of Scripture and tradition, the confession concludes
that "no decrees of popes, or councils, or writings of any person
whatsoever, are of equal authority with the sacred scriptures."[6]

Amid these assertions of biblical authority, the Second London
Confession (1688) acknowledged,

> All things in Scripture are not alike plain in themselves, nor
> alike clear unto all; yet those things which are necessary to be
> known, believed, and observed for Salvation, are so clearly pro-
> pounded, and opened in some place of Scripture or other, that
> not only the learned, but the unlearned, in a due use of ordinary
> means, may attain to a sufficient understanding of them.[7]

While the essential truths of Scripture were "clearly propounded,"
not all aspects of biblical teaching were so easily discerned. Many
early Baptists recognized the complexity of reading, using, and
understanding the Bible even as they insisted that the "unlearned"
could comprehend the text's most basic instruction.

Modernity and the Battles over the Bible

The rise of modern biblical criticism led to extended battles among Baptists (and other denominations) regarding the nature of inspiration. The publication of Darwin's *Origin of Species* was seen by many as a direct challenge to biblical accounts of creation, thereby undermining the veracity of the entire biblical text. It is a controversy that continues into the twenty-first century in debates over creation science. By the late nineteenth and early twentieth century Baptist groups confronted issues of biblical authority related to divisions between Fundamentalists (conservatives) and Modernists (liberals). Biblical inerrancy soon became a major issue for determining orthodoxy related to the nature of biblical inspiration and the nature of the text. Baptist educator David Dockery defines inerrancy as

> the idea that when the facts are known, the Bible (in its autographs, that is, the original documents), properly interpreted in light of the culture and the means of communication that had developed by the time of its composition, is completely true in all that it affirms, to the degree of precision intended by the author's purpose, in all matters relating to God and His creation.[8]

Dockery delineates six particular approaches to biblical inspiration and inerrancy that include,

- *Naïve inerrancy:* God dictated words directly to writers
- *Absolute inerrancy:* Scripture is absolutely true in all matters it discusses
- *Balanced inerrancy:* Scripture is true in all it affirms with the precision intended by writers
- *Limited inerrancy:* Scripture is without error on matters related to faith, doctrine, practice, and ethics
- *Functional inerrancy:* The Spirit will use Scripture to accomplish God's purposes for salvation and transformation of life[9]

Other Baptists insist on the authority of the biblical text without the need to affirm any degree of textual inerrancy. Biblical scholar Walter Harrelson asserts that "historical criticism of the Bible helps the Christian community and its individual believers to pass on the faith intact, seeing to it that the biblical heritage, with all its complexity, variety, and integrity, does not die or atrophy." He maintains that historical criticism "is not merely valuable; it is indispensable if the biblical heritage is to be passed along to the next generation."[10] Baptist theologian Molly T. Marshall urges Baptists "to discriminate between those strands in Scripture, where Scripture most fully bears witness to its focal truth and those strands in which that focal truth is subordinated to lesser concerns." She suggests that the "theology of the cross" is the central hermeneutical principle for understanding Scripture and living out its truths.[11]

More recent studies pursue questions of "Baptist Catholicity" and posit new hermeneutical approaches that link Scripture and tradition, "thick ecumenism," and the pros and cons of postmodern theory in Baptist ecclesiology and biblicism. Such studies are significant and thought-provoking to a fault. But those discussions are not my primary focus in this chapter. Rather, as a historian of the Baptists I am curious as to how their history reflects the use of varying hermeneutical approaches used in confronting textual, cultural, and theological problems.[12]

Representative types of historical Baptist biblicism are evident in a volume titled *The Acts of the Apostles: Four Centuries of Baptist Interpretation*, published in 2009 by Baylor University Press.[13] The book surveys various approaches Baptists have used in interpreting the Bible during their four-hundred-year history. These documents, centered in the Acts of the Apostles, move beyond what Baptists say *about* the Bible to an examination of the varied hermeneutical interpretations they have given to common texts. The sources indicate ways in which the Bible defined Baptists' identity and the ways in which Baptists employed the biblical text itself in response to specific theological and historical contexts across four centuries.

Working with these materials led to questions about the relationship between Baptists' biblicism and their hermeneutic, that is, the ways they interpret and utilize biblical texts. In a work titled *In Search of the New Testament Church: The Baptist Story*, Baptist historian Douglas Weaver writes, "A helpful way to read Baptist history . . . is to say, 'Baptists did this because they believed the Bible or the New Testament church commanded it. Now let's also ask what else was going on that explains why they did what they did.'"[14] One of the things that "was going on" was their method for interpreting the biblical text. By promoting themselves as a biblical people—"the Bible says it, I believe it, and that settles it"—bound by hermeneutical norms, Baptists often painted themselves into assorted theological and cultural corners, sometimes engineering escape by linking biblicism and pietism in creative and quasi-literalist ways.

But what happens when the text will not hold, when individuals or communions inside the Baptist family wear different hermeneutical "glasses" while reading the same biblical passages? What do Baptist churches do when *sola scriptura* and *sola fide* collide? When biblical authority or literalism crashes headlong into piety and practice, culture and conflict, what then? When such theological and cultural dilemmas inevitably occur, many Baptists adapt, even change, their theology, while clinging to the rhetoric of an uncompromised biblicism. And, being Baptists, when such differences occur, they often split, creating new communities gathered around diverse interpretations of pivotal texts. In fact, contradictory readings of common texts divided Baptist groups from the beginning of the movement. Much has been written by and about Baptists and their views on biblical inspiration and hermeneutical theory.

When it comes to the interpretation of ancient texts, University of Chicago scholar David Tracy reminds us, "No classic text comes to us either pure or autonomous. Every classic bears with it the history of its own conflictual history of reception." He encourages "interaction between text and interpreter" by finding "examples where the interpreter is forced to recognize otherness by confronting an unexpected claim to truth."[15] Baptist history offers numerous examples of these textual and hermeneutical dilemmas. A few references from an exceedingly large field of study must suffice.

The Hermeneutics of Contradiction

First, Baptists began amid the hermeneutics of contradiction. The seeds of hermeneutical disagreement and schism were there from the beginning. Indeed, Baptists appear to be the only post-Reformation Protestant community to begin with two contradictory theological perspectives, one Arminian, the other Calvinist. In other words, Baptist origins are characterized by the hermeneutics of contradiction, with groups occupying both ends of the seventeenth-century theological spectrum. The earliest Baptists in Amsterdam and London read the Bible as Arminians, committed to the general atonement, prevenient grace, free will, and falling from grace, doctrines associated with the views of Dutch reformer Jacob Arminius (d. 1609). Convinced that all persons were potentially elected for salvation, they insisted that such election was actualized only through repentance and faith. All who came on those terms were elected to salvation. The English Declaration at Amsterdam (1611) states clearly,

> That GOD before the Foundation of the World hath Predestinated that all that believe in him shall-be saved, Ephes. 1.4; Mark 16.16, and all that believe not shall be damned. Mark 16.16. . . . And this is the election and reprobacion spoken of in the Scriptures, concerning salvacion and condemnacion, and not that GOD hath Predestinated men to be wicked, and so to be damned, for GOD would have all men saved, and come to the knowledge off the truth, I Tim. 2.4.[16]

Through prevenient or enabling grace, individuals freely turned toward Christ whose saving grace cooperated with free will to accomplish regeneration and new birth. Such freedom of the will also meant that the redeemed could turn away from the grace after conversion to Christ.

By the 1630s, a second group of Baptists, Calvinist in doctrine and practice, developed in London and affirmed total depravity, unconditional election, limited atonement, irresistible grace, and perseverance of the saints. The Particular Baptist Confession of 1644 articulates Reformed theology in direct contradiction to the 1611 General Baptist document. It notes,

> That Christ Jesus by his death did bring forth salvation and rec-onciliation onely for the elect, which were those which God the Father gave him; . . . That Faith is the gift of God wrought in the hearts of the elect by the spirit of God, whereby they come to see, know, and believe the truth of the Scriptures.[17]

The hermeneutical differences of these early Baptists are evident in two often overlooked declarations related to the salvation of infants. The General Baptist Orthodox Creed (1679) asserts that

> all little children dying in their infancy, viz. before they are capable to chuse either good or evil, whether born of believing parents, or unbelieving parents, shall be saved by the grace of God, and merit of Christ their redeemer, and work of the holy ghost and so being made members of the invisible church, shall enjoy life everlasting.[18]

The Particular Baptist Second London Confession (1688) insists,

> Elect Infants dying in infancy, are regenerated and saved by Christ through the Spirit; who worketh when, and where, and how he pleaseth: so also are all other elect persons, who are uncapable of being outwardly called by the Ministry of the Word.[19]

Although the New Testament does not explicitly address the question of infant salvation/damnation, the issue was extremely impor-tant in seventeenth-century England given the society's high infant mortality and the Baptist refusal to baptize infants. General and Particular Baptists were compelled to address the topic, extrapolating from Scripture on the basis of their (contradictory) theological positions. The hermeneutics of contradiction then and now mean that while Baptists affirm certain common distinctives, they often interpret them in ways that are not only diverse but also in complete opposition.

The Hermeneutics of Evangelical Inclusion

By the eighteenth century, Calvinist Baptists in Britain (and later in America) modified, in fact changed, their theology in response to an old biblicism and a new globalism springing up around them. William Carey and Andrew Fuller stretched popular theology to the breaking point by promoting the hermeneutics of evangelical inclusion and a biblical mandate to take the gospel to the "heathen," outside England and Europe. In his excellent history of the Baptist Missionary Society, Brian Stanley suggests that prior to the beginnings of the movement Baptists in England were an inward-looking lot with little interest in or plan for global evangelization. Carey and Fuller changed all that.

When Andrew Fuller became the founding secretary of the Baptist Missionary Society in 1792 he insisted, "The object of the society is to evangelize the poor, dark, idolatrous Heathen, by sending missionaries into different parts of the world where the glorious gospel of Christ is not at presently published, to preach the glad tidings of salvation by the blood of the Lamb." He also concluded, "Were these ignorant immortals but thoroughly instructed in the doctrines and precepts of Christianity, their civilization would naturally follow."[20] To more contemporary ears, Fuller's words reflect an evolving approach to evangelism, globalism, and colonialism.

William Carey centered the missionary movement in a biblical mandate, preaching his famous 1792 sermon from Isaiah 54:2-3: "Enlarge the site of your tent, and let the curtains of your habitations be stretched out: do not hold back, lengthen your cords and strengthen your stakes. For you will spread out to the right and to the left." He called British Baptists to look beyond their own shores to those who had "no Bible, no written language . . . no ministers, nor good civil government, nor any of those advantages which we have."[21] Carey and Fuller saw themselves as evangelical Calvinists, following a biblically mandated "duty" to preach the gospel and allowing God to use it to awaken a global elect.

Other Baptists vehemently disagreed. They trusted God to save all the elect, even those (as the Second London Confession says) who were "uncapable of being called by the Ministry of the Word" without human intervention.[22] These Baptists knew that the hermeneutics of evangelical inclusion implied that the entire world could be saved, thereby opening the doors to the general atonement and sounding the death knell of biblically based Calvinism. Thus "Old School" or "Strict Baptists" denied that missionary evangelism was a biblical mandate and rejected the "arrogant pretensions" that "regeneration is produced by impressions made upon the natural mind by means of religious sentiments instilled into it." They insisted that salvation was "exclusively the work of the Holy Ghost, performed by his divine power, at his own sovereign pleasure according to the provisions of the everlasting covenant."[23] For these Strict Baptists, those who promoted an evangelical Calvinist were simply Arminians in disguise. And they were correct. By the early nineteenth century, "Missionary Baptists" had modified, if not changed, their theology of evangelism as illustrated in the New Hampshire Confession of Faith (1833), a document that gave Calvinistic language a decidedly Arminian twist. It reads,

> That Election is the gracious purpose of God, according to which he regenerates, sanctifies and saves sinners; that being perfectly consistent with the free agency of man, it comprehends all the means in connection with the end; that it is a most glorious display of God's sovereign goodness.[24]

The hermeneutics of evangelical inclusion trumped Calvinist biblicism with global conversionism. It introduced the missionary movement into Baptist life, modifying Calvinism in ways that indeed opened the door to the general atonement and a redefinition of election. Ultimately, large numbers of Baptists especially in the American South learned to modify their hermeneutics for evangelism, talking like Calvinists but acting like Arminians.

The Hermeneutics of Cultural Accommodation

In the nineteenth century, Baptists in America divided over the hermeneutics of cultural accommodation clearly evident in the debates over human slavery. At some point in time, probably in response to the Denmark Vesey slave rebellion of 1822 and the rising tide of abolitionism in the North, a significant number of southern ministers came to support chattel slavery using various "biblical defenses" of the South's peculiar institution. Randy J. Sparks concluded that in the early 1800s Baptists and other southern evangelicals realized they could "follow one of two paths: either continue their opposition to the institution [of slavery] and defend the rights of the slaves or restructure their beliefs to accommodate slavery and slaveholders. The first path . . . could destroy the church in the South."[25]

South Carolina pastor Richard Furman was among the first Baptists to articulate that position. As early as 1800, probably in response to Methodist emancipationists in Charleston, Furman advised Baptists, "Rather, therefore, than advocate the speculative, abstract opinions, or attempt the innovations in practice, which on the subject have been advanced and planned by others; let us adhere to these scriptural principles, and perform these duties, so clearly laid down in the volumes of inspiration. On these we may and ought to insist."[26] Furman appealed to Scripture in his most famous address delivered to the South Carolina Legislature in 1822, when he declared,

Had the holding of slaves been a moral evil, it cannot be sup-
posed, that the inspired Apostles, who feared not the faces
of men, and were ready to lay down their lives in the case of
their God, would have tolerated it, for a moment, in the Christian Church. . . . But, instead of this, they let the relationship
remain untouched, as being lawful and right, and insist on the
relative duties. . . . In proving this subject justifiable by Scriptural authority, its morality is also proved; for the Divine Law
never sanctions immoral actions.[27]

Furman urged Baptists and other southerners to adhere to the principles laid out in Holy Scripture for the care of slaves. He suggested
that while slavery and the slave trade were ultimately evil, Afri-
cans "have their situation bettered by being brought here & held as
Slaves, when used as the Scriptures direct."[28]

Soon, the battle over slavery became a debate over biblical
authority with each side claiming the text to support their views on
slavery or abolition. Proslavery supporters moved from St. Paul's
references to slavery in the Epistles to elaborate concoctions from
the Old Testament including the infamous "mark" of Cain and
"curse" of Ham.[29] Opponents of slavery did not hesitate to raise
biblical mandates in support of emancipation. Baptist David Barrow of Kentucky wrote in 1802,

We have an infallible rule. Rom. Xiii: 10. "Love worketh no ill
to his neighbour: therefore love is the fulfilling of the law." But
unmerited, involuntary, perpetual, absolute, hereditary slavery
works the greatest ill to our neighbour, because it deprives him
of every thing, that is near and dear to a rational creature in this
world. . . . If holding a fellow creature in such a state, and treat-
ing him in such a manner (when it is in my power to do otherwise) be to "Love him as myself," and to "do to him as I would
he should do to me"; then I must confess, I neither understand
our Saviour, his prophets or apostles.[30]

Antislavery Baptists appealed to the spiritual truths implicit in biblical commands to love one's neighbor while proslavery Baptists utilized biblical mandates to support an economic and political system. Indeed, Furman concluded that to oppose slavery was "to abandon the Bible or make it teach an expediency."[31]

The Hermeneutics of Liberation

Slaves, it seems, challenged the hermeneutics of cultural accommodation with their own hermeneutics of liberation, reading beyond the declarations of their masters to the biblical stories of deliverance ("Didn't my Lord deliver Daniel, then why not everyone?") and the promise of judgment on the oppressor ("O Mary, don't you weep, don't you mourn, Pharaoh's army got drowned, O Mary, don't you weep"). Likewise, the liberation found in faith and baptism, discovered in the stories of the Bible and in the experience of salvation, carried slaves to a hermeneutical alternative to that offered in many white churches. Nowhere is that more evident than in the simple statement of the slave woman named Winney, a member of the Forks of Elkhorn Baptist Church in central Kentucky. The church minutes of January 1807 report that her owner, Sister Esther Boulwares, brought a "complaint" against her "for saying she once thought it her duty to serve her Master & Mistress but since the lord had converted her, she had never believed that any Christian kept Negroes or Slaves." Sister Boulwares even extended the complaint against Winney "for saying she believed there was Thousands of white people Wallowing in Hell for their treatment to Negroes—and she did not care if there was as many more."[32] That woman talked free. Her hermeneutic of liberation suggested that literalist biblicism was trumped by the social implications inherent in a Conversionist grace. Salvation brought liberation for slaves and the certainty of judgment for slave holders. The minutes of February 1807 report, "The Complaint refer'd last Meeting against Sister Boulwares Winney taken up. She is Excluded [meaning put

out of the church] for the same."[33] A slave woman who called her
Baptist church to live out the power of conversion was excommunicated from a community of faith bound by the hermeneutics of
cultural accommodation.

The hermeneutics of cultural accommodation arose more recently
in questions related to the role of women in Baptist churches, specifically women's ordination. A 1984 resolution at the Southern
Baptist Convention described the issue that continues to divide
many Baptist groups. It outlined specific biblical verses that "exclude
women from pastoral leadership (1 Tim 2:12) and preserve a submission God requires because the man was first in creation and the
woman was first in the Edenic fall (1 Tim 2:13ff)." The resolution
recommended,

> We cannot decide concerns of Christian doctrine and practice
> by modern cultural, sociological, and ecclesiastical trends or by
> emotional factors; that we remind ourselves of the dearly bought
> Baptist principle of the final authority of Scripture in matters of
> faith and conduct; and that we encourage the service of women
> in all aspects of church life and work other than pastoral func-
> tions and leadership roles entailing ordination.[34]

In 2000, Southern Baptists made this view normative for their
churches through a revision of their denominational confession of
faith, the Baptist Faith and Message. It notes, "While both men and
women are gifted for service in the church, the office of pastor is
limited to men as qualified by Scripture" (1 Tim 2:9-14, 3:1-15,
4:14; Col 1:18).[35]

These documents indicate that any deviation from a literal
interpretation of certain biblical mandates would be a clear accommodation to "modern cultural, sociological, and ecclesiastical
trends," a direct repudiation of Baptists' biblicism. However, other
Baptists responded that there were multiple ways of interpreting
biblical texts on these issues. For example, St. Paul broke down

barriers between males and females as well as other divided groups. The activism of women is evident in the Gospels and the Epistles. The Holy Spirit was poured out on "all flesh" at Pentecost, enabling members of both sexes to prophesy. Conversion and baptism are equalizers that open the door to the calling and action of both men and women in the life of the gospel.[36] Indeed, if conversion to Jesus Christ does not destroy "all condemnation," then the power of the gospel may be significantly compromised. Some Baptists have chosen to ordain women to the pastoral office and call them to service in the church. Conversionism leads them to ask, if women were too cursed to be called, might they be too cursed to be saved? On these issues one side's biblicism is another's cultural accommodation and vice versa.

The Hermeneutics of Piety

Finally, no conversation about Baptist biblicism can conclude without reference to the hermeneutics of piety as illustrated in Baptists' approach to the Temperance Movement and the use of wine in communion (and everywhere else for that matter). As the Temperance Movement gained momentum, Baptists continued to insist on following a literal interpretation of Scripture regarding baptism by total immersion, but many relinquished such literalism when it came to the use of wine in the Lord's Supper. Many early Baptists imbibed but shunned the immoderate use of alcohol. Run out of Virginia, Baptist preacher Elijah Craig even invented bourbon on the Kentucky frontier. Nineteenth- and twentieth-century Baptists in America switched from wine to Welch-aid (Mr. Welch invented it for that purpose) and from common cups to shot glasses in response to demands from the Woman's Christian Temperance Union, revival preachers, Social Gospel advocates, and other antiliquor antagonists. They soon moved from temperance to total abstinence where spirits were concerned. Lengthy treatises were composed denying that the "wine" made at Cana or used at the

Last Supper was a fermented beverage. Pietism trumped literalism as temperance clergy and laity rightly pointed to the family abuse, poverty, debauchery, and dehumanization caused by excessive use of alcohol.

Since no one could really say when moderation turned to excess, many Baptists chose to give it up altogether. Christians who wanted to preserve their personal and communal witness, redeem souls and society, and nurture their bodies as the "temple of the Holy Ghost" took "the pledge" declaring that they would abstain from all use of alcoholic beverages.[37] Indeed, the *Temperance Bible-Commentary*, published in 1868, insisted, "It is against the principle of scriptural and moral analogy to suppose that the Saviour exerted His supernatural energy to bring into being a kind of wine which had been condemned by Solomon and the prophets as 'a mocker' and 'defrauder,' and which the Holy Spirit had selected as an emblem of the wrath of the almighty."[38] Even those who, however grudgingly, acknowledged that the Bible did not completely forbid the use of spirits often advised against it for those true Christians who wanted to live above reproach.

Still, many Baptist literalists struggled with biblicism and piety, especially regarding the use of wine in communion. Even some Southern Baptist leaders demurred when it came to grape juice. In 1916, Louisiana Baptist pastor M. E. Dodd wrote,

> So intense has been the feeling and the passions of men concerning the Supper of the Lord that they have even come to the most strenuous contention concerning the elements that should be used. Now everybody is agreed that it should be unleavened bread, for bread with leaven in it, which has the elements of death, cannot represent the pure, spiritual, sinless body of Christ. But we have not been agreed to use the particular character of the fruit of the vine. I have always been of the opinion that it ought not to be grape juice but ought to be

pure, fermented wine. . . . If that is the teaching of our Lord
and the early church practiced it, and when we find what the
Word of God says about it, we ought not to yield one iota from
its teachings.[39]

Primitive Baptists were, as usual, more direct. Some saw it as
another move away from biblical authority by the folks in town.
In his study of Primitive Baptists in Appalachia, John G. Crowley observes, "The use of fermented wine, usually made by the
deacons, is unquestioned among the Primitives." He references a
Primitive Baptist preacher who "once remarked that the Missionary [Baptist] and Methodist use of grape juice in communion was
quite appropriate, since their doctrines bore the same resemblance
to truth as grape juice bore to wine."[40]

Biblicists like the Primitive Baptists and, more recently, conservative Baptist bloggers challenge the hermeneutics of piety by
noting that while temperance and personal abstinence have biblical precedents, total abstinence as an absolute biblical norm is an
isogetical interpretation at best. In a half-hearted response to those
issues, certain Baptist progressives have enacted communion ritu-
als that utilize a common cup with grape juice inside, a thoroughly
unbiblical and pathetically unsanitary via media. Perhaps those
Christians who wish to be sacramentally "biblical" might consider
receiving immersion with the Baptists and then joining the Roman
Catholics, the Anglicans, the Lutherans, or the Primitive Baptists.
Nonetheless, questions of total abstinence from alcohol offer a classic illustration of the way in which Baptists have negotiated literalism through appealing to spirituality.

Baptists and the Bible: A Hermeneutical Pluralism?

What does this hermeneutical pluralism mean for contemporary Baptist life? Several brief observations encourage continuing
dialogue.

- First, Baptists began with a group of seventeenth-century Protestants who were haunted by the text of Scripture and struggled mightily with the meaning of *sola scriptura* and its implications for *sola fide*.
- Second, biblical hermeneutics is neither a simple nor primarily academic pursuit. It is a dangerous necessity undertaken implicitly or explicitly by every Baptist congregation and individual. Biblical hermeneutics sent Baptists to jail and to the mission field. Certain hermeneutics also sent them to the slave auctions. Interpreting the text is terribly dangerous then and now.
- Third, no theory of biblical inspiration or analysis is adequate to make (in the words of the Second London Confession) "all things in Scripture" "plain in themselves" or "clear to all." Theories about the text cannot protect Baptists (or anyone else) from the power and unpredictability of the text itself.
- Fourth, like all other Christian communions Baptists interpret the Bible in light of text and tradition. Denying that reality is a sure path to historical hubris and theological confusion.
- Fifth, from their earliest history, Baptists developed a theological and ecclesial system that creates certain "Baptist ways" for negotiating the "hard sayings" of the biblical text. That system often carried Baptists into "cultural captivity" but also inspired prophetic, dissenting responses grounded in the power of individual and communal conscience. From a historical perspective, Baptists are Biblicists except when they are not. Then they often split.
- Finally, we might conclude with this question: what issues are Baptists currently claiming with biblical and hermeneutical certainty that they will be compelled to apologize for in a century or two? (Recent apologies for sanction-

ing slavery and segregation are a case in point.) After all, the Bible may say it, and Baptists may believe it, but, historically speaking, that does not always settle it! The text haunts us yet.

ONCE SAVED, ALMOST SAVED
Revisiting Baptists and Conversion

※

In 1609 John Smyth and Thomas Helwys led a small group of English expatriates in forming the first Baptist church in the world, constituted around faith and baptism by triune affusion (pouring water on the head three times). In 1610 the group took another action that was to become classically Baptist: they split, with Smyth and others seeking membership with the Waterlander Mennonites and Helwys retaining leadership of the Baptist remnant. A year or so later, shortly before returning to England, Helwys and the Baptists published a Declaration of Faith of English People Remaining in Amsterdam in Holland. In this early confession they set forth the concept of a believers' church, the hallmark of Baptist identity. It declared,

> That the church off CHRIST is a compainy off faithful people I Cor. 1.2. Eph. 1.1. separated fro [from] the world by the word & Spirit off GOD. 2 Cor. 6, 17. being kint [knit] unto the LORD, & one unto another, by Baptisme. 1 Cor. 12.13. Upon their owne confession of the faith. Act. 8.37. and sinnes. Mat. 3.6.[1]

In that simple statement the first Baptists united membership in the church with a "personal profession of faith" ("and sinnes"), distinguishing themselves as a unique type of Protestant community. Today Baptists the world over would surely agree with that statement, at least in principle. But in practice, many Baptist groups lack consensus on what it really means to confess one's faith. If Baptists past and present require that the church be composed of a regenerate membership, what do they mean by regeneration, and how does one secure it?

Defining Conversion

During their first four hundred years, Baptist groups and individuals have offered multiple interpretations of the meaning of Christian conversion, defining the nature of salvation through a variety of doctrines, plans, programs, and personal experiences. Indeed, Baptists' salvation history is indelibly locked into such phrases as "profession of faith," "experience of grace," "getting saved," "being born again," "trusting Christ," "inviting Jesus into your heart," "praying the Sinner's Prayer," "becoming a Christian," "walking the aisle," and "being washed in the blood of the Lamb."

The call for salvific regeneration was not new to the Christian Church when Baptists finally appeared on the scene. Conversion narratives abound from the earliest days of the church. Simply say the words "Damascus Road" and the detailed drama of human transformation comes immediately to mind in the conversion of St. Paul. Paul himself was present at the conversion of the Philippian jailer, whose cry echoed through many a Baptist revival meeting: "Sirs, what must I do to be saved?" Three hundred years later St. Augustine read St. Paul's admonition to "put on the Lord Jesus Christ and make not provision for the flesh," and at that moment, as he says, "all the darkness of doubt vanished away." St. Francis of Assisi heard the words of Jesus at mass in the little church of San Damiano, commanding him to sell everything, give to the poor, and take up the cross of Christ. St. Teresa of Avila confessed her faith when confronted by the *ecce homo*, the statue of Christ bleeding and crowned with thorns. The slave woman named Isabella saw Jesus on a cloud and received from him a new name, Sojourner Truth. Half a century ago, Presbyterian preacher and writer Frederick Buechner heard the phrase "and great laughter" in one of George Buttrick's sermons at Madison Avenue Presbyterian Church and was changed forever.[2]

Yet not everyone reports such dramatic encounters with the divine. Across the centuries many Christians came to faith less by discernable conversion experiences than through what New England preacher Horace Bushnell called "Christian nurture," the churchly growth toward Christian discipleship. William James documented those "once-born" individuals, nurtured to faith through the sacramental grace of the church and never conscious of a time when they were apart from grace.[3] The biblical writer celebrates such "sincerity" of faith in the young Timothy, "a faith that lived first in your grandmother Lois and your mother Eunice, and now, I am sure, lives in you" (2 Tim 1:5). So when did Christians, at least some of them, make a conversion experience normative for all who would claim membership in Christ's church? Rather late in Christian history, so it seems.

Roman Catholic theology then and now linked salvation to the sacramental life of the church, welcoming newborns into the world with the grace of baptism and carrying them through life with the sacraments of confirmation, Eucharist, penance, vocation (marriage or holy orders), and extreme unction. Dramatic conversions might occur among the faithful, but they were in no sense required for participation in the saving grace of Christ present in the church. For Catholics, direct encounter with God was experienced in the sacraments but especially through the Eucharist. Through the miracle of transubstantiation the faithful could literally receive the very body and blood of Christ transformed from bread and wine on the altar by the duly ordained successor of the apostles.

The Protestant Reformation began in part as a response to the Catholic sacerdotal system and a belief that genuine faith was undermined by an ecclesial system centered not in Christ but in papal authority, materialism, and practices outside biblical norms. Wherever else the Reformation took Martin Luther, it began with his very tangible challenge to the indulgence seller Johann Tetzel who showed up in backwater Wittenberg, promoting his own form of Prosperity Gospel. Luther's response made *sola fide* a watchword of the Reformation through his own experience of Romans 1:17, "The one who is righteous shall live by faith." In number thirty-three of the *Ninety-Five Theses* (1517) Luther as usual takes no prisoners, declaring, "Those who think themselves sure of salvation through their letters of pardon [indulgences] will be damned for ever along with their teachers."[4]

Of the corruption of the sacrament of penance, Luther wrote,

> The first and fundamental evil of this sacrament is that they have wholly abolished the sacrament itself, leaving no trace of it. For, like the others, it consists in two things: on God's side, a word of promise, on ours, faith. They have overthrown both of these. . . . They do not speak of the saving faith of the people, but babble solely of the unlimited power of the pontiff, although Christ always acts through faith, not through power.[5]

Amid these denunciations of the papal system, Luther continued to define the church in medieval terms as the dispenser of sacraments received and nurtured by faith. His retention of Christ's Real Presence in communion makes it possible for Lutherans to receive the risen Christ by faith through both the physical and spiritual body and blood of the Savior. Luther denounced those Reformers who denied the physical presence of Christ in and through the bread and wine. John Calvin spiritualized Christ's presence out of the bread and wine and away from Luther's literalism, while Ulrich Zwingli re-formed it into a faith-based but highly intellectualized memorial that combined Reformation piety and Renaissance humanism.

By the time the Baptists appeared on the scene, second-generation Protestants confronted a major question, perhaps not anticipated by the earliest Reformers. If faith alone is necessary for salvation, and if the sacramental signs of Christ's immediate presence are minimized or undermined, how do common sinners know that grace has come to them? The conversion experience made the objective theological idea that God loves human beings and wants to save them tangible in the subjective spiritual life of specific individuals. Through faith in Jesus Christ sinners could know that grace has come to them and salvation is secured.

Baptists began as a distinct religious community by requiring a profession of faith of every individual who would claim membership in the church and developing a congregational process for affirming (or denying) that profession. John Smyth and Thomas Helwys apparently brought these ideas with them from seventeenth-century Puritanism, grounded in Reformed (Calvinist) theology. John Calvin calls regeneration "the commencement of the spiritual life."[6] He wrote that God "begins the good work in us by exciting in our hearts a desire, a love, and a study of righteousness, or (to speak more correctly) by turning, training, and guiding our hearts unto righteousness; and he completes this good work by confirming us unto perseverance."[7] Yet Calvin and the Puritans retained infant baptism as a sign of the covenant of grace, given as a means of grace for the elect. Later Puritans, however, came to insist on a conversion experience of all who would claim such election into grace.

By 1610 John Smyth acknowledged his debt to the "brethren of the separation" (Separatist Puritans), who understood the church as constituted by "sayntes only." The church on earth was to be composed only of professing believers, not the multitudes in a given geographic region who happened to have received infant baptism as mandated by church and state. Seventeenth-century English Puritans inside and outside the Anglican Church placed great emphasis on the need for personal conversion. As the Yale historian Sydney Ahlstrom wrote,

> Whether or not the Puritan made conversion experiences normative, he always regarded the Christian faith as a decisive,

renovating commitment. Anglo-American Puritanism is in fact the fountainhead of a new conception of evangelical inwardness, a type of piety in which the unmerited and purely gracious work of divine mercy in the human soul becomes a cardinal fact of Christian existence.[8]

In many Puritan congregations personal conversion became an increasingly normative experience that set the boundaries for church order and the centrality of covenant relationships. In England and America, those who sought membership in Puritan churches were often required to declare their personal faith, a statement that was then accepted or rejected by the congregation of believers. This process was the beginning of a covenant with God and the believing community. Ahlstrom concluded,

> A specific conversion experience was at first rarely regarded as normative or necessary, though for many it was by this means that assurance of election was received. Gradually, as Puritan pastors and theologians examined themselves and counseled their more earnest and troubled parishioners, a consensus as to the morphology [or process] of true Christian experience began to be formulated. In due course—and with important consequences for America—these Nonconforming Puritans in the Church of England came increasingly to regard a specific experience of regeneration as an essential sign of election. In New England and elsewhere "conversion" would become a requirement for church membership.[9]

This understanding of the nature of conversion constituted the foundation of what came to be known as the Believers' Church Movement, congregations composed only of those who were able to testify to conversion—an experience of divine grace—for themselves.

Baptist Approaches to Conversion

Seventeenth-century Baptists, born of Puritan Separatist, Non-Conformist, Anabaptist mentoring and religious dissent, were quick to affirm the need for a regenerate church membership. They insisted that true members of the church were "visible saints," individuals who knew that they had experienced divine grace in this world as a sign of their salvation now and in eternity. However, early Baptists went beyond Puritans in rejecting infant baptism (a sign of coerced faith) in favor of the baptism of believers only.

The Standard Confession of General Baptists, published in 1660, describes the nature of conversion quite clearly. It states that the way to justification is

> by faith in Christ, Rom. 5.1. That is to say, when men shall assent to the truth of the Gospel, believing with all their hearts, that there is remission of sins, and eternal life to be had in Christ. And that Christ therefore is most worthy [of] their constant affections, and subjection to all his Commandments, and therefore resolve with purpose of heart so to subject unto him in all things, and no longer unto themselves, 2 Cor. 5.15.[10]

For those Arminian Baptists, saving faith involved acknowledging the truth of the gospel, accepting forgiveness of sins through Christ, subjecting themselves to Christ's commands, and maintaining a "purpose of heart" to live beyond themselves. It is a superb statement of the process of Christian conversion.

Likewise, the Orthodox Creed (1679), another General Baptist document, notes that those who are "united unto Christ by effectual faith, are regenerated, and have a new heart and spirit created in them through the virtue of Christ his death, resurrection, and intercession, and by the efficacy of the holy spirit, received by faith."[11] Believers' baptism was the outward and visible sign of a believers' church. Infants, incapable of such a cathartic experience, were not appropriate subjects for faith or baptism. In linking conversion experience directly with adult baptism, Baptists parted company with those Puritans who retained infant baptism as a "sign of the covenant." They also separated themselves from an establishmentarian ecclesiology, the union of church and state that compelled the baptism of all infants in a given country or region.

While these early Baptists agreed on the need for a regenerate church membership, they often divided over the morphology (process) of or constituency for salvation. Their earliest communions, known as General and Particular Baptists, occupied opposite ends of the theological spectrum regarding issues of grace and free will, election and predestination. They differed on who could be saved and how salvation was secured.

General Baptists, on the scene by 1608–1609, were Arminians who insisted that all persons were potentially elected to salvation and could actualize that election by repentance and faith. Prevenient or enabling grace permitted sinners to exercise their free will in accepting God's saving grace. Enabling grace and saving grace cooperated together to accomplish salvation. For General Baptists, regeneration followed repentance and faith. Christ's death on the cross was a general atonement, offered for the sins of the entire world. If persons had the free will to receive Christ, they had the free will to reject Christ along the way. The Standard Confession notes,

> That such who are true Believers, even Branches in Christ the Vine, . . . or such who have charity out of a pure heart, and of a good conscience, and of Faith unfeigned, I Tim. 1:5, may nevertheless for want of watchfulness, swerve and turn aside from the same, verse 6, 7, and become as withered Branches, cast into the fire and burned, John 15.6. But such as add unto their Faith Vertue, and unto Vertue Knowledge, and unto Knowledge Temperance, &c. 2 Pet. 1.5-7, such shall never fall . . . verse 8-10.[12]

For General Baptists, "falling from grace" was a real possibility for those who had once chosen Christ and received regeneration. The fallen had once experienced "unfeigned" or genuine faith but had allowed themselves to turn from their earlier commitment. They had chosen to turn their backs on the grace they had once received.

Particular or Calvinistic Baptists, developing out of English Independency in London in the 1630s, insisted that regeneration preceded repentance and faith, made possible only by the infusion of grace into the heart of totally depraved but elected individuals. Only after God imparted grace into the sinner's heart did he or she have the free will to repent and believe in Christ. God's grace also enabled the elect to persevere to the end. Christ's death on the cross was a limited atonement, applicable only to the elect, chosen before the foundation of the world.

The Second London Confession (1677/1688) of Particular Baptists states, "The Grace of Faith, whereby the Elect are enabled to believe to the saving of their souls, is the work of the Spirit of Christ in their hearts; and is ordinarily wrought by the Ministry of the Word." The Confession suggests that through the infusion of grace the depraved sinner "is enabled to cast his Soul upon the truth thus believed; and also acteth differently, upon that which each particular, [biblical] passage thereof containeth; yielding obedience to the commands, trembling at the threatenings, and embracing the promises of God, for this life and that which is to come."[13]

For these Calvinist Baptists, those whom grace calls, grace keeps eternally. Election is unconditional and does not depend on the whims of the individual. Those whom grace redeems may sin along the way but will ever be brought to repentance. The Second London Confession declares,

> Those whom God hath accepted in the beloved, effectually called and sanctified by his Spirit, and given the precious faith of his Elect unto, can neither totally nor finally fall from the state

of grace; but shall certainly persevere therein to the end and be eternally saved. . . . This perseverance of the Saints depends not upon their own free will; but upon the immutability of the decree of Election, flowing from the free and unchangeable love of God the Father.[14]

Again, both General and Particular Baptists affirmed the need for a regenerate church membership but disagreed significantly on the theology and process of regeneration itself. General Baptists insisted that repentance and faith preceded regeneration, while Particular Baptists believed that regeneration preceded repentance and faith.

These distinctions in conversion processes are extremely important for understanding the evolution of the conversion experience in Baptist life, particularly in the United States. While both approaches were present in the earliest Baptist congregations in the New World, the Calvinist position dominated early on. As the country moved across the West and revivalism gained momentum on the frontier and in burgeoning urban areas, Conversionist preachers gave greater emphasis to freedom of the will, the general atonement, and the cooperation of saving faith and free choice in the salvific process. They used the language of Calvinism but within the context of a more Arminian approach to the nature of salvation.

America: Multiple Conversion Morphologies

In America, Baptist understanding of conversion was shaped by religious awakenings and revivals from New England to the Kentucky frontier. The movement known as the First Great Awakening brought numerous converts into the churches along with divisions over the role of religious affections or "enthusiastical" religion as signs of a genuine conversion experience. Jonathan Edwards, the great Puritan pastor and theologian, was among the first persons to document the conversion morphologies he observed when an awakening struck his church in Northampton, Massachusetts, in 1734–1735. Indeed, Edwards' treatise, *A Faithful Narrative of the Surprising Work of God*, is perhaps the first real case study on awakenings to be published in America. In it he describes in detail the conversion of two women, one—Abigail Hutchinson—converted on her deathbed and the other—Phoebe Bartlet—converted as a four-year-old. Since persons were totally depraved from their mother's womb, grace could fall upon the elect whenever and at whatever age God might choose, even at an early age. Edwards defined conversion as

> a great and glorious work of God's power, at once changing the heart, and infusing life into the dead soul; though that grace that is then implanted does more gradually display itself in some than in others. But as to fixing on the precise time when they put forth the very act of grace, there is a great deal of difference in different persons; in some it seems to be very discernable when the very time of this was; but others are more at a loss.[15]

As a revival swept the church and the community, Edwards documented the process he observed as sinners came to repentance. The revival ended almost as abruptly as it had begun due in part to the attempted suicide of one of Edwards' own relatives, whom he describes as "a poor weak man" "who being in great spiritual trouble, was hurried with violent temptations to cut his own throat, and made an attempt, but did not do it effectually."[16]

With the decline of revival sentiments, Edwards then published his observations in the *Faithful Narrative*. As he saw it the conversion process involved the following elements: (1) a sense of dependence on God's "sovereign power," (2) deep conviction of sin and helplessness at overcoming it, (3) terror over one's lost condition, and (4) a sense of God's justice in condemning the totally depraved sinner. In time, however, those who were truly elected began to recognize the graciousness of the divine as revealed in Jesus Christ and to express gratitude toward God that such grace had found them. With that thankfulness, the sinner recognized and acknowledged the hope of salvation.[17] Ironically, Edwards' observations became for many the actual method for evaluating true and false conversions, thereby making salvation less surprising and more predictable as one charted the proven steps.

Like other Protestant groups, Baptists were divided over numerous aspects of the awakening, primarily related to worship and the role of emotions in the conversion experience. Regular Baptists retained a staunch Calvinism, continued to sing the Psalms as the divinely appointed hymnody, and called ministers with worthy educational credentials. They demanded conversion of all church members but resisted revival methods of mass evangelism and enthusiastical religious experience. Separate Baptists, on the other hand, gladly participated in the awakening, singing "man-made" hymns and gravitating toward preachers who could preach with boldness regardless of their educational credentials or lack thereof. Separate Baptists got saved hard, often with great emotion. While their preachers affirmed Calvinist language, their preaching tended to open the door to the possibility that all their hearers could choose salvation. In the aftermath of the First Great Awakening Baptists themselves developed conflicting plans of salvation, sometimes with serious skepticism as to the validity of varying morphologies.

Revivalism became even more pronounced as the churches moved west. Baptists were frequent participants in the camp meetings and "protracted" revivals of frontier church life and the Second Great Awakening. Indeed, from the mid-nineteenth to the late twentieth century, revivals became a major venue for Baptist evangelism and conversion theology. Revivals shortened the process of conversion, fostered "intense individualization" of religious experiences, extended conversionistic emotionalism, and shaped simple plans of salvation that were easily preached and appropriated. In short, revivalism created a theology of conversion and a methodology for securing it that shaped Baptist life to the present day. Nineteenth-century evangelists such as Presbyterian Charles G. Finney and Baptists Jabez Swan and Jacob Knapp called sinners to the "anxious bench," an area in the church or meeting hall where those "under conviction" could come in order to be aided toward conversion. Traditional Calvinists said it smacked of works righteousness, offering false security to sinners who mistakenly believed that there was something they could do to make salvation happen. Revivalists countered by insisting that was simply a "means" for opening the gates for repentance and faith on the spot.

The anxious bench was surely the precursor of the "invitation to Christian conversion and discipleship" that remains a part of much Baptist conversion liturgy, a time at the end of the service when persons are urged to "come forward" to receive Christ as savior or recommit their lives to Christian living. Revivalists called the unsaved to walk the aisle as an outward and visible sign of an experience of new birth. The ingredients of salvation in these settings included faith, submission, repentance, and a conscious decision to follow Christ. Finney wrote, "There is great variety in people's [conversion] exercises. Whatever point is taken hold of, between God and the sinner, when the sinner YIELDS, he is converted."[18] For Finney and other revivalists, God's primary purpose for all humanity was salvation, and the sooner the better in each individual.

In his *General History of the Baptist Denomination in America*, published in 1813, David Benedict wrote, "From 1799 to 1803, there were, in most parts of the United States, remarkable outpourings of the Divine Spirit, among different denominations; multitudes became the subjects of religious concern, and were made to rejoice in the salvation of God. The revival among the Baptists in the southern and western States . . . [brought] astonishing additions to their churches."[19] As members joined the churches, methods were developed for moderating the individualism of the conversions through the participation of the congregation. Individualistic conversion was tempered by communal/congregational affirmation, indeed approval. In most Baptist churches, those who sought membership were required to testify to their conversion and the congregation was then asked to vote as to its perceived validity. Historian Paul Harvey describes these processes, noting,

> Church boards and elders routinely challenged the validity of the conversions, often requiring greater proof of the experiences of the candidates for membership. As a northern Baptist discovered, supposed converts who went before the church "with an intelligent Christian experience" were not rewarded but rather "sent back to seek further, until they [came] with the usual stranger visions and physical demonstrations.[20]

He reports that one Virginia Baptist church determined that a would-be convert did not "understand her self [sic] or the Principles of Christ's dealings with his people." Thus the church voted to ask her to return "to a Throne of God's Grace which is able to make her wise unto devotion."[21]

If Baptists could vote converts into the church they could also vote them out, so the confirmation of conversion and admission to membership was a reminder of the covenant between God and the believer as well as between the believer and the congregation. To break the covenant was to face the possibility of expulsion or "churching," an action frequently taken by nineteenth- and early-twentieth-century Baptist churches.

This practice of voting on conversions is still evident today in the tepid reception often given to those who walk the aisle in Baptist churches across the South. When people come forward for baptism or membership, ministers often ask the congregation, "If you favor admitting/welcoming this person to our church please signify by the uplifted hand." If a negative vote is entertained at all it often goes something like this: "All those opposed by the same sign, and of course there are none." Converts are seldom asked to relate their "experience," and most congregations would never think of rejecting any converts. Conversionist individualism prevails.

Conversion as Transaction

As revivalism became institutionalized in congregations and evangelistic crusades, certain public and private processes were established for securing salvation and certainty. Over time, salvation often became associated with a particular spiritual or transactional formula centered in the Sinner's Prayer and made public by walking the "sawdust trail" of a tent revival or the aisle of a church. A. C. Dixon, prominent Baptist preacher of the early twentieth century, insisted,

> In dealing with an inquirer when you *see* that he has come to the point of accepting Christ, it is well to ask him to kneel with you and pray aloud. His prayer will be an index to his heart. If he begins with confessing sin and thanking God for the gift of Christ, you may be sure that he is saved. If he apologizes for sin and fails to make a full confession, he needs further instruction.[22]

"Evangelistic" sermons and gospel tracts delineated the "plan of salvation" that suggested "if you have done your part (believe that Christ died in your place and receive him as your savior and master), God has done his part, and imparted to you His own nature." By the mid-twentieth century, the Sinner's Prayer became the centerpiece of mass revivalism and conversionism for audiences large and small. A recent Internet version mirrors the tradition by asking sinners to pray,

> Lord Jesus, I know that I am a sinner, and unless you save me I am lost forever. I thank you for dying for me at Calvary. I come to you now, Lord, the best way I know how, and ask you to save me. I now receive you as my Savior, in Jesus Christ [*sic*] name. Amen.[23]

In the book *Those Who Came Forward*, Curtis Mitchell described a scene at a typical Billy Graham crusade in which the evangelist led those seeking conversion "through a short prayer of repentance and confession. They repeated it, two thousand voices so soft they could hardly be heard. Then, as Graham turned to depart, the battalions of converts changed into a new formation, presenting an amazing picture."[24] In many respects, there is no clearer illustration of the union of public profession of faith and Sinner's Prayer than in the work of Billy Graham.

Conversion and Once Saved, Always Saved

What became a normative methodology for securing salvation clearly brought redemption, new life, and Christian commitment to multitudes of individuals, many of whom moved into churches across the country and around the world. Yet as in past periods of awakening, explanations as to "how to be saved" shaped the popular theology of what salvation meant. As conversion morphologies were adapted for massive crowds or shortened into less theologically cumbersome explanations, several issues took shape.

First, conversion turned from a surprising work of God into a salvific transaction centered in a highly propositional formula for securing divine grace. The mystery of an "enthusiastical" encounter with the divine became a basic assent to a highly intellectualized statement of or request for faith. Justification, entering into salvation, became the central, in some cases perhaps the only, Christian experience. Indeed, many Baptists placed so much emphasis on justification that sanctification—going on in grace—was minimized, nearly ignored. As Samuel Hill and Dennis Owen concluded of late-twentieth-century conversionism, "It is as if we have produced consumers of the born-again movement, frozen in the hour they first believed. It is rather like being in love with falling in love."[25] As conversion became static, many Baptists have gravitated toward aspects of the Charismatic Movement with its emphasis on experiential religion, sanctification, and a quest for continuing or deepening experiences of God's grace.

Second, perhaps there is no clearer illustration of the impact of transactional conversionism on Baptist theology and practice than the doctrine of "once saved, always saved," a bit of theological doggerel that evolved into a powerful, if problematic, affirmation of faith. At first glance, the phrase seems a simple way of explaining the Calvinistic dogma of the perseverance of the saints, a belief described in the London Confession of Particular Baptists in 1644. It states,

> Those that have this precious faith wrought in them by the Spirit, can never finally nor totally fall away . . . but shall be kept by the power of God to salvation, where they shall enjoy their purchased possession, they being formerly engraven upon the palms of Gods [sic] hands.[26]

Perseverance meant that, although redeemed persons might indeed "fall into grievous sin, and for a time continue therein . . . yet they shall renew their repentance and be preserved through faith in Christ Jesus to the end."[27] Thus did the elect endure in Christian living, kept by grace and moving from faith to faith amid the inevitable struggles with sin.

As the concept worked its way into popular parlance, "once saved, always saved" minimized perseverance and maximized the initial entry into grace. Once individuals prayed the "Sinner's Prayer," exercised their free will, and invited Jesus into their hearts, God was compelled to save and salvation was secured forever. While perseverance was preferred, it was not necessary to ultimate salvation. Some even suggested,

> Our salvation is secure—even if we believe NOT after we are saved, because we become part of him (Body of Christ) . . . and "he abideth faithful: HE cannot deny himself." 2 Tim. 2:13.[28]

Christian faith and practice could come or go but God was obligated to save. Salvation was less a gift than an entitlement once the necessary transaction was complete. The idea of "once saved, always saved" is a fascinating case study in the evolution of conversion morphologies in Baptist history. Originally intended as a synonym for perseverance of the saints, it perpetuated a view of conversion that was more contract than covenant. Completing the transaction became the primary, if not the only, responsibility of sinners seeking eternal security. Yet as "once saved, always saved" worked its way into popular Baptist piety, especially in the American South, what began as a source of assurance often contributed to an abiding doubt. Doubts arose as to whether the transaction was completed, the right prayer prayed, or the right concepts in place to create a valid regeneration experience. In fact, in some Baptist quarters, the rebaptism of multitudes of previously "born-again" individuals illustrates the presence of doubt among people schooled in "once saved, always saved" assurance. The result has been a significant confusion as to the idea of a believers' church and the nature of conversion itself. In many churches, the same people are born again, again and again.

Baptists and the Future of Conversionism

In the first decade of the twenty-first century, what does conversion mean for Baptists, and what are they to do about it? Several observations prompt dialogue, I believe.

First, as Baptists enter their four hundredth year it is time to revisit a theology of regeneration. In America, the waning of revivalism as a mechanism for evangelistic conversion and the rise of multiple conversion processes require churches to reexamine the nature of regeneration and conversion in light of Scripture, history, and popular culture.

Second, it is clear that transactional conversionism remains a major force among those who call themselves evangelicals inside and outside the Baptist family. Yet the theological and pastoral problems of transaction conversionism must be confronted if we are to reexamine the nature of conversion itself.

Third, new morphologies of conversion have already worked their way into the evangelical and Baptist ethos. Even a brief survey illustrates the multiple choices now available. "Possibility thinking" conversionism views sin as a poor self-image and conversion as a method for thinking better of your true self. Prosperity conversionism uses the language of revivalism while demanding that God provide the redeemed with healing and wealth, not as a miracle given inexplicably to some but as an entitlement claimed by all. A renewed Calvinism insists that elect individuals are able to respond to grace only after it is infused from outside their totally depraved human nature. Television evangelists often suggest that salvation is simply a motel prayer that settles everything and sends born-again sinners on their way to heaven, no muss, no fuss. Individualistic conversionism distances itself at least implicitly from an essential connection to Christian community. Spirituality conversionism leads some persons to shop around from tradition to tradition, religion to religion, eclectically drawing on a variety of religious insights. Given these multiple methods, how will Baptists articulate the meaning of a believers' church?

Fourth, new voices, many raised in response to this evangelical confusion, are evident in the contemporary, postmodern church. This is particularly evident in the so-called Emerging Church Movement and its insistence that personal salvation is inseparable from covenant community—a strangely seventeenth-century Baptist idea. Salvation is itself an abidingly sacramental process, nurtured not in rabid individualism but in communal humility. Emerging Church analysts such as Eddie Gibbs and Ryan K. Bolger observe,

> The gospel of emerging churches is not confined to personal salvation. It is social transformation arising from the presence and permeation of the reign of Christ. . . . Emerging churches

are no longer satisfied with a reductionist, individualized and privatized message.[29]

Likewise, Emerging Church leader Joel McClure writes,

> The gospel is not that we agree with some abstract propositions in order to qualify to go to heaven when we die but an invitation to live in a new way of life. Sharing the good news is not only about conversion. It is about inviting someone to walk with you relationally, and it takes a while to demonstrate this gospel![30]

Those words echo the affirmation of that scruffy group of exiled and schismatic Puritans, reconstituting the church as best they understood it in Amsterdam in 1609 and declaring,

> That the church off CHRIST is a company off faithful people I Cor. 1.2 Eph. 1.1 seperated from the world by the word & Spirit off GOD. 2 Cor. 6.17. being kint unto the LORD, & unto another, by Baptisme. I Cor. 12.13. Upon their owne confession of the faith. Act 8.37. and sinnes. Mat. 3.6.[31]

The words of the Orthodox Creed call Baptists to reclaim the dynamic community of a believers' church:

> There is one holy catholic church, consisting of, or made up of the whole number of the elect, that have been, are, or shall be gathered, in one body under Christ, the only head thereof; which church is gathered by special grace, and the powerful and internal work of the spirit; and are effectually united unto Christ their head, and can never fall away.[32]

In such a community individuals cast themselves on Christ, trusting him to offer grace and carry it to the end according to grace alone. If Martin Luther called pious Christians of his day to look beyond the crass transactionalism of the sixteenth-century indulgence sellers, so we must do the same in the twenty-first-century church, recovering the meaning of *sola fide*, casting ourselves on Christ and living out his gospel in the world.

6

A CONGREGATIONAL SACRAMENTALISM
Revisiting Baptist Ecclesiology
※

Previous chapters have already confirmed that early Baptist identity was characterized by emphasis on biblical authority, regenerate church membership, believers' baptism by immersion, congregational church polity, religious liberty, and the priesthood of all who claim faith in Christ. Amid those initially separatist, ultimately sectarian characteristics is an enduring legacy centered in (to repeat) the importance of uncoerced faith grounded in the power of conscience and the inevitability of dissent. Make no mistake about it: those who founded the first Baptist church in Amsterdam in 1608–1609 moved from Puritan separatism to Baptist sectarianism when they relinquished identification with the established church and its union of baptism with citizenship. Believers' baptism, first by trine affusion (pouring) and then by immersion, was a public profession of faith in Christ, an acceptance of the covenant of church membership, and a dangerous act of dissent against "normative," culture-bound, state-privileged Christianity.

Baptists understood conscience and dissent in light of the need for sinners to be regenerated, made new through conversion to Christ. Yet in their assertion that conscience could not be compelled by either state-based or faith-based establishments, they flung the door wide for religious liberty and pluralism in ways that even they did not fully comprehend. Believers' baptism, ultimately by immersion, was thus a radical act of Christian commitment, covenantal relationships, and antiestablishment dissent. A believers' church publicly manifested in believers' baptism was characterized by a congregational sacramentalism, in which the congregation of believers united to Christ and one another by baptism, was itself an outward and visible sign of an inward and covenantal grace.

Conscience and religious liberty were not based on secular theories (although they would ultimately impact them) but on the necessity of uncoerced faith uniting the converted with a congregation of Christian believers. A commitment to freedom of conscience led Baptists to oppose religious establishments and develop principles of religious liberty that anticipated modern pluralism.

Baptists were dissenters from the very beginning. They challenged political and religious establishments in a variety of ways. First, they were nonconformists who often rejected the religious uniformity for faith-based support demanded by the state-based churches of their day. Second, they rejected any laws of church or state that compelled financial or liturgical compliance for a religious communion in which they had no voice. Third, they defied any church or state that legislated belief by virtue of birth, economic status, or culture privilege and separated themselves from it. Thus they were exiled, jailed, and otherwise endangered.

Anglican priest Daniel Featley's description of seventeenth-century Baptists illustrates the basis of their radical nonconformity. Featley's list of Baptists' beliefs as he understood them revealed an establishmentarian nightmare. It also provides insight into how seventeenth-century dissenters were perceived by their religio-political enemies. Featley described Baptists as follows:

> First, that none are rightly baptized but those who are dipt. [They rejected the socially and politically mandated mode of baptism.]

Secondly, that no children ought to be baptized. [They cast aside the link between baptism and citizenship—rejecting the idea that to be born into a "Christian" state required immediate baptism into the official state church.]

Thirdly, that there ought to be no set form of Liturgy or prayer by the Book, but onely by the Spirit. [They demanded the freedom to determine their own spirituality apart from governmental majority-enforced prayer.]

Fourthly, that there ought to be no distinction by the Word of God between the Clergy and the Laity but that all who are gifted may preach the Word, and administer the Sacraments. [They challenged the status of a privileged religious class that controlled theology, liturgy, and admission to the sacraments.]

Fifthly, that it is not lawful to take an oath at all, no, not though it be demanded by the magistrate. [The oath reflected the loyalty of citizenship. Many early Baptists would swear only to God, not governments, but later Baptists gave that up.]

Sixthly, that no Christian may with good conscience execute the office of civil magistrate. [They knew, did they not?][1]

Every article in this fascinating list reflects degrees of nonconformity among Baptists theologically, liturgically, and politically. Their dissent had clear political and religious implications. Truth is, being Baptist was never all that respectable. As their earliest critics saw it, Baptists demonstrated bad theology, bad citizenship, and bad manners every time they opened their mouths.

Such dissent was also evident in New England in conflicts between Baptists and the Puritan establishment. Roger Williams, the brilliant proto-Baptist, was exiled into the "howling wilderness" of New England in 1636 for preaching "the same course of rigid separation and anabaptistry" as the Baptists in "Amsterdam had done."[2] He made it worse by insisting that the Native Americans were the owners of the American land and should be justly compensated for it. In exile, Williams purchased land from the Narragansetts, writing, "I having made covenant of peaceable neighborhood with all the sachems and natives round about us, and having, in a sense of God's merciful providence unto me in my distress, called the place Providence, I desired it might be for a shelter for persons distressed of conscience. . . . I communicated my said purchase unto my loving friends . . . who then desired to take shelter here with me."[3] Let me be very personal here. I find those words—"a shelter for persons distressed of conscience"—one of the most amazing phrases I have ever read, the hallmark of religious liberty and human courage. They haunt me almost every day of my life and are as relevant today as they were almost four hundred years ago.

Although Williams himself soon left the Baptist fold, other Baptists understood the relationship of faith and conscience as insightfully as he did. Listen to this rather lengthy passage from the 1678 Orthodox Creed, one of the most dynamic summaries of the genius of early Baptist ideals ever written. It states,

> That the Lord Jesus Christ, who is king of kings, and lord of all by purchase, and is judge of quick and dead, is only Lord of Conscience; having a peculiar right so to be. He having died for that end, to take away the guilt, and to destroy the filth of sin, that keeps the consciences of all men in thralldom, and bondage, till they are set free by his special grace. And therefore he would not have the consciences of men in bondage to, or imposed upon, by any usurpation, tyranny, or command whatsoever, contrary to his revealed will in his word, which is the only rule he hath left, for the consciences of all men to be ruled and regulated, guided by, through the assistance of his spirit. And therefore the obedience to any command, or decree, that is

not revealed in, or consonant to his word, in the holy oracles of scripture, is a betraying of the true liberty of conscience. And the requiring of an implicit faith, and an absolute blind obedience, destroys liberty of conscience, and reason also, it being repugnant to both, and that any man, can make that action, obedience, or practice, lawful and good, that is not grounded in, or upon the authority of holy scripture, or right reason agreeable thereunto.[4]

The phrase "And the requiring of an implicit faith, and an absolute blind obedience, destroys liberty of conscience, and reason also, it being repugnant to both" is a dramatic illustration of Baptists' commitment to the power of conscience. It was the call to uncoerced faith that produced the appeal to conscience and the necessity of dissent. It was the witness of the permanent minority, a group of people amazed that their views would be acknowledged this side of the kingdom of God but who demanded voice and conscience nonetheless.

But the early Baptists did not stop there. They went beyond their Puritan colleagues to reenact a radical sacrament/symbol of that free faith—believers' baptism, ultimately by immersion. I believe that such radical faith, radical conscience, radical baptism, and radical dissent are worth revisiting, debating, and somehow claiming in the permanent transition that lies ahead of us in the church and in the world. We are all indebted to a variety of scholars, especially younger scholars, who have raised these questions of Baptist identity, faith, and baptism in the past few years. These include British professors such as Anthony Cross, Paul Fiddes, Ian Randall, and Toivo Pilli, as well as Philip Thompson, Pam Durso, and Baylor colleagues Beth Barr, Doug Weaver, Mikeal Parsons, and Barry Harvey.

Baptism remains the outward sacrament/sign that links regenerate church membership, conscience, and dissent as the central witness of Baptist identity in the world. In short, believers' baptism does many things for the individual and the community of faith. First, it is a biblical act, identifying the believer with Jesus and the movement he called the kingdom of God. The English Declaration at Amsterdam (1611) said it plainly:

> That everie Church is to receive all their members by Baptisme upon the confession of their faith and sinnes wrought by the preaching of the Gospel, according to the primitive Institution. Mat. 28.19.[5]

It is that biblical mandate that united and divided the first Baptist church in the world, in 1609 prompting John Smyth to baptize himself and then the others who gathered in Amsterdam. But the quest for the most biblical form and theology of baptism led to the first Baptist split with Smyth's decision to seek a truer baptismal authority with the Mennonites. Thus Baptist commitment to baptism as a biblical act is the most enduring source of Baptist unity and division.

Second, believers' baptism is a conversion act, demonstrating the new birth of an individual and incorporating that individual into Christ's body, the church. Again, the English Declaration says it simply: "That Baptisme or washing with Water, is the outward manifestacion of dieing unto sinn, and walkeing in newness off life."[6] For those early Baptists baptism was public profession of faith. It still is.

Third, believers' baptism is a churchly act that marks the entry of believers into the covenantal community of the church. Baptism, while administered to individuals, is not an individualistic act. It is incorporation into Christ and his church. Remember that wonderful description of the church set forth by the earliest Baptists in 1611?

> That the church off CHRIST is a company off faithful people
> I Cor. 1.2 Eph. 1.1 seperated fro(m) the world by the word
> & Spirit off GOD. 2 Cor. 6, 17. being k(n)it unto the LORD, &

one unto another, by Baptisme. I Cor. 12.13. Upon their owne confession(n) of faith. Act. 8.37 and sinnes Mat.3.6.[7]

This is a short but powerful summary of the covenantal relation of believers with God and with one another.

Fourth, believers' baptism was and remains a dangerous and dissenting act that frees Christian believers to challenge the principalities and powers of church and culture in response to the dictates of conscience. Clearly, this was the case at the beginning of the movement four hundred years ago. Believers' baptism required a complete break with the state-privileged church and its identification, indeed enforcement, of baptism and citizenship. It set Baptists at odds with the Puritan/Presbyterian separatists who birthed them but retained infant baptism as a New Testament counterpart of circumcision. While not all the seventeenth-century confessions address conscience's radical impact on matters of church and state, some confront it head on. The Standard Confession of 1660 acknowledges the need for "civil Magistrates in all Nations," but warns,

> in case the Civil Powers do, or shall at any time impose things about matters of Religion, which we through conscience to God cannot actually obey, then we with Peter also do say, that we ought (in such cases) to obey God rather than men . . . and purpose, that (in such cases) in the least actually obey them; yet humbly to suffer whatsoever shall be inflicted upon us, for our conscionable forbearance.[8]

That wonderful, terrifying confession leads me to this recapitulation. Four hundred years into the history of the movement Baptist identity remains grounded in the idea of the uncoerced faith of a believers' church, gathered to Christ by baptismal immersion, living out of conscience and the unending possibility of dissent for the sake of a dangerous and death-defying gospel. If that is so, then what are we to do about it on the way through the twenty-first

Interesting → Tradition Instituted on Disturbance Sacrament has Forgotten Sacramentalism.

century? Clearly, we need to revisit our hermeneutics—how we read and use the Bible—and our conversionism—how we understand and articulate the meaning of a believers' church. Baptists, especially in North America, should revisit believers' baptism as the great faith-based, dangerous, sacrament-symbol-ordinance of our gospel identity in the world. At its gospel best, therefore, baptism is the great outward and visible sign of an inner and covenantal grace in every era—ancient, modern, and postmodern.

If baptism is that significant, and if we revisit our current theologies and practices surrounding it, how will we deal with the two most pressing baptismal problems confronting many contemporary Baptist congregations: rebaptism of nonimmersed long-term Christians and the rebaptism of Baptist church members? In a sense, these questions are case studies for the Baptist future in considering the three topics of this chapter: biblicism, conversionism, and ecclesiology in a Baptist context.

First, the rebaptism of persons previously baptized as infants but seeking membership in a Baptist congregation is perhaps the oldest and most historically divisive question in the history of the movement. Baptist churches are on "safe" historical ground if they have either open or closed baptismal policies. Second, the rebaptism of large numbers of Baptist church members in certain congregations compels churches to confront issues related to the baptism of children, the nature of conversion, and the theology of baptism itself. Revisiting baptismal theology and practice compels churches to ask these, among other, questions:

- Do those churches that accept baptism from other traditions have a way of incorporating new members liturgically and "covenantally" into a believers' church? Might a renewal of baptismal vows become a public profession of long-held faith in a new community of the faithful?
- Can churches that require immersion of nonimmersed, long-time Christians articulate a clear biblical mandate for

doing so, especially when ~~"New Testament baptism" is~~ given
to those ~~who have made immediate profession of~~ faith?

- Does immersion given to long-term Christians on the basis of a profession of faith require recipients to repudiate at least implicitly their earlier faith and the Christian tradition that nurtured them to grace?
- Should immersion of long-time Christians at least be distinguished from the immersion of new converts?
- Given that infant baptism is no longer mandated by state-based religious establishments, are Baptist churches that require immersion of all members prepared to declare that the churches from which would-be members come are "false churches" (early Baptists' word) or "mere societies" (Old Landmark word)?
- Given that the New Testament knows nothing of child baptism, can Baptist churches that require immersion of all members claim "the true New Testament baptism" if they baptize persons under the bar/bat mitzvah age of twelve?
- Given that many Baptist churches accept children—some even in the preschool ages—how will they define the nature of a believers' church?
- More importantly, perhaps, if Baptist churches are going to baptize children, especially very young children, can they commit themselves to what theology professor Frank Tupper calls "Mediated Memory," helping children to remember their profession of faith and baptism? Can they develop clear, intentional methods for "confirming" the faith of children once they confront the moral and spiritual dilemmas of adolescence and adulthood?
- What can some Baptist churches do to extricate themselves from the cycle of rebaptism given multiple times to professing Christians? If baptism is administered in the name of God, Father, Son, and Holy Spirit, when does rebaptism become an act of literally taking the name of God in vain?

- As Baptists lose their culture-dominant status, how does baptism become a renewed sign of conscience and dissent in the world?
- How might Baptist churches again become, in the words of Roger Williams, "a shelter for persons distressed of conscience" and a prophetic community that distresses the consciences of members and nonmembers alike in response to the great issues, ideas, and injustices of our times?
- Might the early Baptists' radical understanding of conscience encourage us to an equally radical concern for voice—an environment in which everyone can speak even when the differences are vast and irreconcilable?
- Finally, might a recovery of Baptist dissent compel Baptists to articulate ideas that inform and challenge the church and the culture, even when they will never secure majoritarian approval?

An example of that dissent in response to national and global issues was illustrated just a few weeks ago in a prophetic document written not by a Baptist but by Reverend Maria Bonafede, moderator of the Tavola Valdense, a community of Waldensian Churches in Italy. Titled "The Responsibility of a Minority," it expresses vigorous opposition to the efforts of the Italian government to fingerprint 80,000 Rom-Gypsy children in Italy, a mistaken attempt to respond to crime, anti-immigrant and antigypsy sentiments in contemporary Italian society. Reverend Bonafede offers this powerful explanation for her opposition to this practice, words that capture brilliantly the reason why Baptists need to recover faith and conscience in an ever-expanding globalism. She writes,

> There are moments during which responsibility for vigorously affirming fundamental principles of civil society falls on the shoulders of small minorities. It is the duty of these minorities to intervene because they know first hand the pain of prejudice and persecution inflicted by the majority, a majority all

too often ill informed, distracted, confused or manipulated and therefore unable to stop episodes of hatred, discrimination and violence against whomever's turn it is to be different. Today it is the turn of the Gypsy children. . . . As Waldensians and Methodists, we acknowledge ourselves a minority that on the topic of civil rights has an important word to say. We speak, therefore, with all the strength and conviction at our disposal. We cannot keep silent during this moment when our spiritual, ethical and civil responsibility demand we speak out.[9]

Like our Waldensian and Methodist brothers and sisters in Italy and elsewhere, we Baptists have a historic obligation to exercise "the responsibility of a minority," in our cultures and, for many of us perhaps, in our own churches and subdenominations, speaking out from the depth of Christ-arrested consciences to "hatred, discrimination and violence" of our global communities.

As a historian, I am impressed by the courage and dissent that characterized the congregational sacramentalism of the earliest Baptist communities of faith. We owe a great debt to those sixteenth- and seventeenth-century dissenters obsessed with conscience and voice for heretic and atheist alike. They spoke out because they could not remain silent, whether anyone paid much attention to them or not. Indeed, as a religious community, Baptists have never done well with privilege, whatever form it takes. Parson Woodmason was right then and now; we do not all "agree in one tune," you see, it is a matter of conscience.

7

TOWARD A BAPTIST FUTURE
The Challenge Ahead

If Baptists are a case study in denominational transition in twenty-first-century America, then great challenges lie ahead for all Protestant traditions as churches, boards, agencies, schools, and other institutions confront the period of permanent transition that has descended on religious bodies across the nation and around the world. Contemporary congregations, whether thriving or declining in membership, focused or distracted in their identity, face great challenges related to the nature of the church, the purpose of its ministry, worship, and sacraments, and its sense of mission. New generations of Christians and seekers, many unfamiliar with old traditions and common practices, require knowledge and training, often in the most basic rubrics of the faith.

And if Baptists in general are a case study in such institutional and ideological transitions, Southern Baptists are surely a case within the case. America's largest Protestant denomination (sixteen million by some counts) has engaged in a variety of highly public disputes for more than thirty years. At their annual convention gatherings Southern Baptists consistently address numerous public issues including critiques of the "homosexual agenda," abortion, secularism, theological liberalism, public schools, cussing preachers, and repentance from their own early support of slavery. Conflicts between so-called conservatives and moderates extended to every segment of denominational life from the national convention to local congregations.

For many observers, "The Controversy" that dominated the history of the Southern Baptist Convention (SBC) for decades began at the denomination's annual meeting in Houston, Texas, in June 1979. Although divisions between so-called moderates and conservatives were evident by the 1960s, the Houston Convention marked the first election of a series of denomination presidents who would use their appointive powers to install conservative majorities on the trustee boards of all Convention agencies. These trustees would then promote a "course correction" that would deliver the SBC from the jaws of theological liberalism and confessional compromise. Moderates, on the other hand, viewed this effort as a "takeover" movement that would undermine Convention unity and distract it from its evangelical mission. Adrian Rogers, then pastor of Belleview Baptist Church, Memphis, and a prince of the conservative pulpit, was elected president on the first ballot with some 51 percent of the vote over numerous other moderate candidates. For over thirty years Southern Baptist majorities have elected conservatives who facilitated the doctrinal and practical confessionalism supported by those who desired a "course correction" in the theological life of the denomination. By 1985 conservative dominance of the denominational system was solidly confirmed with the election of Atlanta pastor Charles Stanley as Convention president at an annual convention held in Dallas in the presence of at least forty-five thousand messengers. This represents the largest meeting of the SBC that was ever or undoubtedly will ever be held.

The Controversy was fierce and divisive, impacting every segment of SBC life. Many state Baptist colleges and universities relinquished or significantly redefined their relationship with their respective state Baptist conventions. Faculties at Convention-owned seminaries experienced extensive turnover, with several forced terminations. A greater degree of doctrinal and confessional unanimity came to characterize Convention programs and employment. Trustees were changed, agencies were changed, and the departure or disengagement of moderates was under way. The conservative course correction succeeded in accomplishing its essential goals, but even that success could not stem the tide of statistical decline that descended on the denomination by the early 2000s. The still formidable SBC retains its significant numerical dominance in American Protestantism, but Convention demographics, like those of other Baptist groups, reflect a denomination in a considerable transition, if not outright decline, torn by internal controversies on one side and megachurch competition on the other, held together by an aging constituency, faltering finances, and turbulent identity crises.

Other Baptist denominational groups reflect these demographic realities even if their internal struggles have been less public than those of the SBC. Indeed, while certain congregations are thriving, many Baptist communions across the theological spectrum from liberal/progressive to conservative/Fundamentalist are experiencing general declines in denominational statistics and identity. Inside a new century, Baptists are redefining themselves, disconnecting, reclaiming identity, rejecting identity, or experiencing varying degrees of schism.

Thus Baptists represent a case study in the changing nature of religion and denominations in twenty-first-century American culture. They are at once a sectarian movement standing against culture, fighting "worldliness" in its varied forms while claiming various forms of orthodoxy, and a culture-bound Protestant establishment, incorporating elements of the culture and often seeking to dominate it.

Toward a Baptist Future: A Time of Transition

Would the seventeenth-century Baptists recognize the faith and practice of contemporary Baptist churches? No doubt they would, even from a significant theological and cultural distance. Indeed, many contemporary debates and divisions over issues such as baptism, salvation, and authority mirror those that were present at the beginning of the Baptist movement. Given current transitions and continuing differences, how might Baptist history inform Baptist identity in the present and, more importantly, toward the future?

First, transitions in American religious culture, clearly evident but often ignored in the twentieth century, are now normative in many Baptist communities. For example, Baptist groups across the geographical, racial, and theological spectra often seem in a continued state of reorganization in response to declining membership, waning finances, and the loss of denominational loyalty. Many Baptist congregations wear their denominational connections rather loosely, picking and choosing resources and services. Some have even begun to "franchise" themselves, connecting with struggling churches throughout their respective regions and essentially taking them over, re-forming them with a new pastoral minister, and linking them to the "mother church" through the electronically manifested image of the senior pastor and preacher.

Statistical decline seems to have settled on most if not all denominations in the Baptist community in the United States. Indeed, in 2009, both the SBC and the American Baptist Churches, USA were presented with new proposals for reorganizing cumbersome denominational structures that inhibit rather than enable ministry possibilities and funding realities.[1] National Baptist groups are revisiting their hierarchies as well, struggling together to deal with the African American megachurch phenomenon radically affecting their denominational constituencies and statistics. Primitive and Old Regular Baptist groups, many of which are based in Appalachia, are now experiencing serious numerical decline related to changes in family demographics and the long-term hesitancy to engage in direct evangelism. Independent Baptists, long known for their Fundamentalist separatism and antagonism toward charismatic piety, now demonstrate a greater openness toward spiritual gifts and contemporary forms of worship that they once denounced as "worldly." At the same time, certain Baptist churches continue as if nothing has changed, promoting traditional denominational alignments, retaining older forms of worship, and sustaining classic forms of doctrinal orthodoxy. Others are claiming or reclaiming historical traditions, particularly Calvinism or certain elements of Reformed theology. Indeed, Calvinism is one of the highlights of theological specificity and renewal in numerous segments of Baptist life in the United States.

In many instances a de facto society method characteristic of earlier Baptist organizations has settled into the uneasy relationship between local Baptist churches and their varying "associational" networks, allowing congregations to support selected denominational programs. Baptist churches, conservative, moderate, and liberal, continue to renegotiate their "Baptistness," creating various connections to old denominational organizations and identities.[2] In short, changes in technology and ecclesiology mean that local congregations no longer need denominations as they once did. Many now generate their own educational literature, mission emphases, funding, and theological education for members alongside and apart from official denominational systems. Churches have learned to participate in certain denominational programs while ignoring others. Whether the "society method" of specialized individual and congregational connectedness is a long-term option or simply a stopgap effort on the road to complete organizational collapse remains to be seen.

Second, while regional, economic, and racial divisions remain, a new generation of Baptist clergy and laity find themselves working and worshiping together in distinct and creative ways evident in changing neighborhoods, interracial relationships, community organizing, ecumenical networks, and charismatic spirituality. Efforts to incorporate new cultural modes of music, technology, and communications in retelling "the old, old story of Jesus and his love" are present in Baptist churches across a wide theological spectrum. Younger Baptists, many affirming distinctly conservative doctrines, now testify to the spiritual benefits of "Christian heavy metal" music and "theology on tap." Theological conversations and debates are renewed daily on Facebook, Twitter, and innumerable Web-based blogs.

New ecclesiological approaches seem increasingly normative. Elements of megachurch or emerging church ideology and methodology have also found their way into Baptist congregations, many of which are not mega or have never emerged from much of anything. Many congregations of varying theological and liturgical orientations have dropped or minimized the name Baptist, fretting that it scares people off, sounds too sectarian, or has become synonymous with bigotry or compassionless dogmatism. Many Baptists, left and right of center, observe that "brand-name" religion no longer attracts.

Third, new coalitions of Baptists offer multiple options for interchurch cooperation and ministry relationships. These include the Alliance of Baptists (1987), the Cooperative Baptist Fellowship (1990), Texas Baptists Committed (1988), the Association of Welcoming and Affirming Baptist Churches (1993), the Association of Reformed Baptist Churches of America (1997), and the Spurgeon Baptist Association of Churches. Many of the churches linked to these organizations often retain dual alignment with other Baptist groups such as the SBC or the American Baptist Churches, USA, while others have broken those traditional ties completely. Among African American Baptists, various national Baptist groups such as the National Baptist Convention, USA, the National Baptist Convention of America, the Progressive National Baptist Convention, and the National Missionary Baptist Convention, often at odds in the past, have begun to hold occasional gatherings for common worship and cooperative conversations. These events might never have occurred were it not for the impact of African American megachurches on the old denominational systems.

In January 2008 some seventeen thousand Caucasian, Latino, and African American Baptists met in Atlanta for the New Baptist Covenant conference organized under the leadership of former president and Baptist Sunday school teacher Jimmy Carter and a Steering Committee composed of leaders from a variety of Baptist denominations and churches. This was the largest gathering of African American, Caucasian, and Latino Baptists ever held in the United States. In 2009 a variety of New Baptist Covenant regional meetings were held throughout the country, further extending the new network. The future of this coalition remains to be determined.

Younger members—under age forty or so, male/female, black/white/Hispanic—were not reared in the days of intact denominational systems. If they have a sense of Baptist identity at all it is probably formed around a specific local congregation. Many have a limited frame of reference for understanding how and why Baptists practice immersion, call ministers, maintain congregational polity, and use temperance grape juice in communion. Many of these young people eschew sectarian divisions for a kind of generic Christianity, highly individualized, often charismatic, and almost always less denominationally oriented. Many reflect a transitional ecclesiology that is a synthesis of denominational, congregational, megachurch, emerging church, and postmodern approaches to ministry. If Baptist identity is to be carried beyond midcentury it must be reasserted, reinterpreted, and re-formed—and none too soon.

Fourth, years of controversy over Scripture, doctrine, and politics among many Baptist groups have often obscured significant theological problems that extend denominational and congregational uncertainties. Two examples must suffice. Obsession with theories of biblical authority and inspiration has often masked serious questions of biblical hermeneutics—how the text is interpreted—and kept the text itself at a distance from readers who try to protect its veracity rather than explore its wonder. An increasing biblical illiteracy is evident in churches left and right of center. Whatever else Christian postmodernism may mean, it is surely sending some people into the biblical text in ways that seem to invigorate and renew. Indeed, in her work on *The Great Emergence*, Phyllis Tickle writes that the contemporary church must "formulate—and soon—something other than Luther's *sola scriptura* which, although used so well by the Great Reformation originally, is now seen as hopelessly outmoded and insufficient, even after it is . . . spruced up and re-couched in more current sensibilities."[3] Tickle believes that a renewed authority is to be found in both Scripture and community, linked inextricably in a "network" relationship. She insists, "The end result of this understanding of dynamic structure is the realization that no one of the member parts or connecting networks has the whole or entire 'truth' of anything, either as such and/or when independent of the others." Tickle concludes, "Neither established human authority nor scholarly no priestly discernment alone can lead, because, being human, both are trapped in space/time and thereby prevented from a perspective of total understanding. Rather, it is how the message runs back and forth, over and about, the hubs of the network that it is tried and amended and tempered into wisdom and right action for effecting the Father's will."[4] Tickle's concern for a renewed relationship between individuals and communities reflects something of the early Baptist concern for similar covenantal connections in a believers' church.

Likewise, changes in evangelistic theology and method have left a variety of Baptists uncertain as to what conversion means, how it is experienced, and what are the most effective methods for declaring the gospel in an increasingly secular, postmodern culture. Multiple methods for receiving salvation dominate the airwaves of religious media, creating uncertainty as to how, when, and on what route conversion occurs. The complex issues of child conversion in a denomination that touts a believers' church remain unexamined by many Baptist groups. The implications of a transactional conversionism in which one prays a "Sinner's Prayer" that enables believers to be "once saved, always saved" have received limited theological reflection in many Baptist congregations. All this contributes to what seems an evangelical confusion about the nature of conversion, the significance of believers' baptism, and the meaning of faith itself. In short, for all their rhetoric about the Bible and regeneration, Baptists as a group often seem uncertain as to how those truths are applied and understood.

Finally, Baptists now confront the dilemma of their denominational "image" in the public square. On one level they seem the ultimate sectarian movement, toeing the doctrinal and ethical line on a wide variety of issues. On another, they appear to be the epitome of denominational identity, an old-guard religious majority in Protestant America. As denominational divisions and declines gain momentum, Baptists confront the loss of varying degrees of cultural input and privilege. Nonetheless, one of the great strengths of Baptist churches is their diverse ministries, their care of souls, and their willingness to serve persons inside and outside the church. Strategies for church growth and energizing faith communities begin with basic pastoral care for those who are hurting, dying, starving, and homeless. The effective witness of any congregation is grounded in its service to persons in Christ's name.

Toward a Baptist Future: Covenant Communities

What in the Baptist heritage and vision offers insight toward the future? Perhaps some clues, past and present, might be found in the Declaration of Faith of English People Remaining in Amsterdam in Holland (1611), a basic confession of faith written by the Amsterdam community just before some of them headed back to England and certain persecution. Their astute ecclesiology might be helpful in shaping twenty-first-century Baptist communities. It is an astounding document that defines the church as follows:

> That the church of Christ is a company of faithful people separated from the world by the word and spirit of God being knit

unto the Lord and one unto another, by baptism, upon their own confession of the faith.[5]

These Baptists believed that churches were to be organized around a covenant with Christ as accepted by those who could testify to a direct experience of God's grace through faith. While many within Puritanism made conversion normative for all who would claim church membership, they also retained infant baptism. Baptists insisted that baptism must follow a confession of faith as a sign of uncoerced redemption and a direct encounter with the divine. Commitment to a church of confessing believers is a central tenet of early Baptist ecclesiology. Contemporary Baptists are heirs of that commitment.

Toward the future, Baptists might reassert that emphasis on a believers' church while reexamining and re-forming the meaning and nature of regeneration theologically, individually and communally.

- Early Baptists blended individual salvation with churchly affirmation through covenant with God and with the community of faith. Personal conversion accounts were offered to the congregation or their representatives who determined whether they were genuine enough for admission to church membership. The church often received the statement of faith of individual believers on the basis of congregational approval. Members thus confirmed the veracity of the individual's conversion experience. The approval of a covenant relationship also meant that the congregation had disciplinary responsibility when members stepped outside the covenant. That tradition, now extensively modified or largely lost, remains a historic reminder of covenantal commitments and relationships. Contemporary Baptist churches might decide to reassert the link between individual faith and communal relationships, and congregational autonomy means that each congregation has the freedom to develop those relationships as seems best in particular contexts. Some congregations may place more emphasis on the church's disciplinary responsibility, calling members to take seriously their commitments to faithful living and ordered discipleship. Others may become entry points for persons already disciplined by life's inequities or their own difficult (or bad) choices, offering grace to those who need extensive healing before they can even begin to confront the cost of discipleship. Still others may place covenantal relationships in the context of service to church or community. Other congregations will surely struggle with elements of those and other approaches to the nature of covenants.

- In an earlier era, revivals and other evangelistic efforts created a context for conversion that became increasingly normative in Baptist churches. As those mechanisms have changed or vanished, Baptist churches need to again confront the meaning of regeneration, conversion, and a believers' church. Churches could become more intentional about utilizing multiple morphologies (processes) for conversion that would include such venues as direct evangelism, pastoral care, friendship and fellowship, worship, and service as ways to reinvigorate the witness of the church. Indeed, in America revivalism was a creative response to the "barbarism" of a rapidly expanding frontier environment. While those methods seem increasingly less effective in an increasingly urban nation, the opportunity for creativity remains essential. Some of the most successful congregations in terms of effective ministry and spiritual vigor are those that have found a peculiar niche in their unique settings.

- Over much of the twentieth century, many Baptists moved toward a transactional form of evangelism—praying Sinners' Prayers, signing "decision cards," and claiming individual and immediate entry into salvation. While such an approach offers a clear and concise method, it may also contribute to a quantitative act that undermines lifelong discipleship, makes salvation a one-time and immediate entitlement, and stresses the power of the human over against the divine.

In the four hundredth year of their history Baptist churches and individuals might revisit the nature of regeneration, the meaning of a believers' church, and the process of salvation that involves both justification, entering into faith, and sanctification, going on in grace.

Toward a Baptist Future: Reaffirming Believers' Baptism

And then there is baptism. The Declaration at Amsterdam states "that Baptism or washing with Water, is the outward manifestation of dying unto sin, and walking in newness of life. And therefore in no wise appertaineth to infants."[6] To retain the name Baptist is to revisit biblical, historical, theological, and contextual aspects of the tradition's most distinguishing public characteristic.

Early on, Baptists understood conscience and dissent in light of the need for sinners to be "regenerated," made new through conversion to Christ. Yet in their assertion that conscience could not be compelled by either state-based or faith-based establishments, they flung the door wide for religious liberty and pluralism in ways that even they did not fully comprehend. Believers' baptism, ultimately by immersion, was thus a radical act of Christian commitment, covenantal relationships, and antiestablishment dissent. Conscience and religious liberty were not based on secular theories (although they would ultimately impact them) but on the necessity of uncoerced faith uniting the converted with a congregation of Christian believers. A commitment to freedom of conscience led Baptists to oppose religious establishments and develop principles of religious liberty that anticipated modern pluralism.

Contemporary Baptists would do well to reconsider baptism as the outward sacrament/ordinance that links regenerate church membership, conscience, and Christian commitment as the central witness of Baptist identity in the world. Reexamining the nature and meaning of believers' baptism is especially important given the influx of nonimmersed but long-term Christians who seek membership in Baptist churches and the phenomenon of the rebaptism of Baptist church members who profess faith and receive immersion multiple times.

In his monumental work on *Baptism and the Baptists*, Anthony Cross surveys the history of baptism with particular concern for transitions in contemporary Baptist life. He insists that "the Baptist doctrine and practice of baptism in the twentieth [and twenty-first] century is contextual (something that has only rarely been admitted by Baptists), and that as contexts have changed so too have Baptist baptismal beliefs and practices."[7] In addressing British Baptists, Cross concludes that "there is no single Baptist theology or practice of baptism, only theologies and practices, and this diversity accords with Baptist ecclesiology which continues to tend toward independency each local church and individual minister exercising their liberty in the administration and interpretation of Christ's laws."[8] He insists, correctly, that the context for baptism in Baptist churches has been impacted by a decline in "denominational loyalty" and an "individuality" that places greater emphasis on decision than on "the corporate dimension of the rite."[9] Likewise, in Britain (and in America as well), ecumenical relationships in churches and in families have forced Baptists to reexamine questions of open and closed baptism as persons from varying Christian communions seek to join their number.[10]

In the twenty-first century, believers' baptism accomplishes many of the same theological and spiritual benefits as those known by seventeenth-century Baptists. First, it is a biblical act, identifying the believer with Jesus and the movement he called the kingdom of God. The English Declaration at Amsterdam (1611) said it plainly:

> That everie Church is to receive all their members by Baptisme upon the confession of their faith and sinnes wrought by the preaching of the Gospel, according to the primitive Institution. Mat. 28.19.[11]

It is that biblical mandate that united and divided the first Baptist church in the world, prompting John Smyth to baptize himself and then the others who gathered with him there in Amsterdam. Additional study of Scripture led Smyth to leave the Baptists and seek admission to the Mennonites, whom he believed to have a more appropriate baptismal tradition. Thus Baptist commitment to baptism as a biblical act is perhaps the most enduring source of Baptist unity and division.

Second, believers' baptism is a conversion act, demonstrating the new birth of an individual and incorporating that individual into Christ's body, the church. For those early Baptists baptism itself was public profession of faith. It still is.

Third, believers' baptism is a churchly act that marks the entry of believers into the covenantal community of a specific congregation. Baptism, while administered to individuals, is not an individualistic act. It is incorporation into Christ and his body, the church. It is truly a sign of the covenant of grace in the life of the believer and the believing community.

Fourth, believers' baptism remains a dangerous and dissenting act that frees Christian believers to challenge the principalities and powers of church and culture in response to the dictates of conscience. Clearly, this was the case at the beginning of the movement four hundred years ago. It set Baptists at odds with the Anglican/Puritan establishments in England and America and marked their effort to break the link between baptism and national citizenship that had developed in European churches from the Constantinian era.

Fifth, if baptism is essential to Baptist identity then and now, then churches that are centered in the idea of believers' baptism must revisit their baptismal theology and practices with some regularity. For example, certain Baptist churches have begun instituting the laying on of hands at baptism, a practice established by the early Six Principle Baptists, as a way of highlighting the calling of every person of faith. This act marks the "setting aside" of all believers as ministers of Christ through the power of the Holy Spirit, a sign that in one sense ordination belongs to all who profess faith in Christ.

Toward a Baptist Future: The Nature of the Church

And what of congregational polity in Baptist life? Again, the Baptists exiled in Amsterdam might offer appropriate instruction for twenty-first-century churches. As the Declaration at Amsterdam states,

> That as one congregation hath CHRIST, so hath all. And that the Word of GOD cometh not out from any one, neither to any one congregation in particular, but unto every particular Church, as it doth unto all the world. And therefore no church ought to challenge any prerogative over any other.[12]

For the early Baptists the authority of Christ was mediated through the congregation of believers and each congregation was both free and responsible for the direction of its ministry and the form of its discipleship. Even then, however, these fledgling congregations debated, disagreed, and split over multiple issues of doctrine and practice. Freedom of conscience in every believer did not mean that the congregational majority was compelled to accept all dissenters in their ranks. Recalcitrant members could be voted out by congregational majority. Covenant and discipline shaped the nature of community and congregational interaction. When congregationalism works it is a bona fide "people's movement," enabling the community of faith to move toward common tasks with energy and consensus. When it falters it is a sure mechanism for failure and schism, with limited mechanism for mediation. Congregational polity offers significant latitude to autonomous local churches to explore possibilities for ministry that reflect spiritual imperatives and local responsibilities. Again, twenty-first-century Baptists might confront various questions and issues included as follows:

- Is congregational polity still a viable option for congregations where members are less engaged or where the church itself is too large for serious communal dialogue and interaction?
- In light of denominational disengagements, will individual Baptist churches be compelled to seek new or additional associational relationships that facilitate ministerial placements, interchurch networks, and even assistance in adjudicating disputes?
- As traditional denominational connections diminish, where will churches find resources for understanding and interpreting clergy-laity authority, relationships, and disputes? Will new approaches to the "business model" of church administration (e.g., with the senior pastor as CEO) be developed more extensively?
- Can local congregations develop options for congregational mediation before disputes arise?

Baptist theologian Paul Fiddes understands congregational relationships in terms of the ancient Baptist idea of covenant and the church as "gathered community, a phrase with a double meaning." First, its "members certainly agree to gather"; . . . "the dynamic of an intentional community." Second, the community "is also *gathered* by God. They gather in response to the 'appointment' of Christ, the Lord of the church, who is already gathering them into his one body." This covenanting community, Fiddes believes, is "not just *drawing* together, but *being drawn* together."[13]

If Fiddes' words portray the ideal of a Christian and Baptist community, the reality in many Baptist congregations is all too scandalous. Divisions public and private seem present throughout Baptist life, characterized by general animosity, ministerial terminations, and congregational schism. Indeed, in too many cases, Baptists are often perceived to be a religious communion that "multiplies by dividing," so consistent is their penchant for intrachurch turmoil and a sometimes public airing of their disagreements.

And if Baptist identity is to be passed on into a new century, congregations across the theological spectrum will be compelled to reexamine the nature of their church polity, distinguishing business methods and bylaws from the theological methods of covenant community. Pastors and people must remain open to traditional and nontraditional ways of communicating and ministering together. It is perhaps their most formidable task for the future.

Toward a Baptist Future: Rediscovering the Text

And what about the Bible? Concerning Scripture, the seventeenth-century exiles wrote this simple statement in the Declaration from Amsterdam:

> That the scriptures of the Old and New Testament are written for our instruction, and that we ought to search them for they testify of CHRIST. And therefore [are] to be used with all reverence, as containing the Holy Word of God, which only is our direction in all things whatsoever.[14]

Clearly, the first Baptists were thoroughgoing Biblicists, who would readily change their theology if convinced of a clearer biblical mandate, as evidenced in Smyth's departure to the Mennonites. This brief statement antedates the great debates over biblical authority and hermeneutics related to biblical criticism, biblical inerrancy, and issues raised by modernism, fundamentalism, and now postmodernism. In fact, the innocence of the words is itself disarming. Toward the future, as Baptists continue to look to Scripture for authority and guidance, the following issues might be considered:

- Divisions over biblical authority will continue to characterize Baptist life, enlivening consciences, extending debates,
  and galvanizing faith communities. Are there possibilities
  for common ground and shared ministry even among those
  Baptists who cannot agree on the nature of biblical inspiration and interpretation?
- How will Baptists rediscover the wonder of the biblical
  text amid the continuing debates over the nature of biblical authority?

Toward the future, Baptists will no doubt continue to affirm
biblical authority as central and essential for communities of faith
and individual believers. The church is itself gathered by and around
the word of God, ever teaching, preaching, and learning from its
insights as guided by the Holy Spirit. Amid that commitment, divisions over the nature of biblical authority, theories of biblical inspiration, and the role of hermeneutics show no signs of dissipating in
Baptist life. It remains to be seen where the text and the Spirit will
take Baptists in the century ahead.

Toward a Baptist Future: A Theology for Mission

In a sense, Baptists entered the modern mission movement by
rethinking their theology, rewriting their essentially Reformed
theology to include a mandate to preach the gospel to the world.
In so doing they insisted that although the ultimate salvific benefits
of that preaching were limited to a divinely predetermined elect,
everyone could potentially benefit from the moral order that the
sovereign God willed for all creation. In short, they enlarged their
vision of Christianity's global implications just enough to justify
sending out preachers as agents of God's word and representatives
of Christian civilization. In time, that theology became a wedge that
opened the door of salvation, at least by implication and possibility,
to the entire race. If you preach as if everyone can (potentially) be

saved, sooner or later people will come to believe that everyone can actually do so. Strict Baptists in England and Primitive Baptists in the United States knew that ultimately a "modified" Calvinism was hardly Calvinism at all, hence their opposition to aggressive missionary action and the mission boards that promoted it. For those Baptists such efforts were human efforts to usurp what only God could provide: genuine regeneration born only by divine infusion of grace. Nonetheless, this movement did indeed help to extend Protestant Christianity throughout the world. It inculcated a missionary imperative that is the hallmark of many Baptists' global vision and direct action.

Contemporary Baptists confront a similar theological challenge in the face of a new pluralism with global implications. The challenge begins with the decision to assert the uniqueness of the Christian revelation and the need of all persons to have an "experience with Christ" while responding hospitably to persons who are just as committed to another distinct (and non-Christian) religious tradition. (Similar dynamics are asked of those religions in response to Christianity, it might be noted.) Such global pluralism might mean that Baptists learn to listen closely to representatives of other world religions, even as they acknowledge deep differences regarding the nature of faith and the need for conversion.

Like the Primitive Baptist response to modified Calvinism, certain Baptists may be unable to participate in elaborate interfaith dialogue or a response to the beliefs of other world religions except as a means of responding to their lack of truth. For some Baptists, dialogue with other religions may imply an equality of revelation that they find unacceptable. This dilemma will surely increase as communities and families come into greater connection with devotees of other religions. Developing strategies for this ever-expanding reality is one of the great challenges Baptists must face in the twenty-first century.

Conclusions: An Audacious Witness

Issues of Baptist identity—believers' church, covenant community, individual conscience, biblical hermeneutics, global mission—require considerable study, reexamination, and perhaps even reformation by Baptist groups across the theological spectrum. The early Baptists remain an amazing resource for understanding the nature of the Baptist witness past and present. Their insistence on a church of believers anticipated the future in the Free Church Tradition, radical religious liberty, religious pluralism, and, for some, a global vision for Christianity. They understood that theirs was a minority voice in the world, and they were often willing to stake their lives on it.

Baptists might decide if they want to provide a prophetic witness to American or global societies or retain religio-cultural dominance and privilege. In short, when Baptist groups exercise their dissenting tradition—a noble aspect of Baptist history—they should anticipate divisive responses in the church and in the public square. They must learn how to address the pluralistic public square, recognizing the implications of conscience, conviction, and dissent. In short, what sounds like conviction in a Baptist church can be seen as bigotry in the larger society.

Currently many conservative Baptists cannot seem to decide if they are dissenters, standing against the secularism that they believe to be the unofficial religious establishment of an increasingly antireligious nation, or establishmentarians, demanding a certain kind of religious privilege for their way of believing in a historically "Christian" nation. Moderate/liberal Baptists are so uncertain about their past and future that they cannot seem to decide what, when, or if to protest anything at all. The search for an effective witness continues.

That witness is exactly what the first Baptists knew when in 1611 they dashed off a confession of faith on their way back to England from Amsterdam. It declared,

Though in respect of Christ, the church be one, yet it consisteth of divers particular congregations, even so many as there shall be in the World, every [one] of which congregation, though they be but two or three, have Christ given them, with all the means of their salvation. [They] are the Body of Christ and a whole church.[15]

An audacious witness then; an audacious witness for the future.

NOTES

Preface

1 Edward Bean Underhill, "Historical Introduction," in *The Records of a Church of Christ, meeting in Broadmead, Bristol, 1640–1687* (London: J. Haddon, 1847), xliv. The church was the Broadmead Baptist Church in Bristol, but the name Baptist was not in extensive use in the late 1600s.

2 Peter Cartwright, *The Autobiography of Peter Cartwright* (New York: Phillips & Hunt, 1856), 133–34; emphasis in original.

3 David Crumm, "Call to Worship Starts with a New Church Name," *Detroit Free Press*, April 3, 2000. The four-thousand-member church changed its name from Temple Baptist Church to Northridge Church in 2000.

4 "Baptist Is Our Middle Name," Neuse Baptist Church, Neusebaptist.com/history.

Chapter 1

1 Richard J. Hooker, ed., *The Carolina Back Country on the Eve of the Revolution: The Journal and Other Writings of Charles Woodmason, Anglican Itinerant* (Chapel Hill: University of North Carolina Press, 1953), 109. *see* also John G. Crowley, *Primitive Baptists of the Wiregrass South 1815 to the Present* (Gainesville: University of Florida Press, 1998), 8.

2 "Va. Congressman Fears More Muslims Elected," msnbc.msn.com/id/16311648, December 21, 2006.

3 See godhatesamerica.com. The Westboro Baptist Church in Kansas, with Fred Phelps as pastor, has led a movement to demonstrate at funerals of

persons with AIDS and soldiers killed in Iraq and at lectures of persons they determine to be "prohomosexual."

4   Jonathan Turley, "Minister Prays for Death of President Obama," JonathanTurley.org, June 5, 2009. Turley describes the "imprecatory prayers" of the Reverend Wiley Drake, Baptist pastor and former second vice president of the Southern Baptist Convention. He concludes his article by noting that the Constitution permits free speech, even when asking God to kill people.

5   For a discussion of these varied groups *see* Christopher Hill, *The World Turned Upside Down* (1984; repr., New York: Penguin, 1991).

6   Richard J. Hooker, ed., *The Carolina Back Country on the Eve of the Revolution*, 109.

7   See Converge Worldwide, www.scene3.org/content/view/1924/70/.

8   See godhatesamerica.com and godhatesfags.com for details of the church's approach to homosexuals and the Iraq war.

9   Paul Gifford, "A View of Ghana's New Christianity," in *The Changing Face of Christianity: Africa, the West, and the World*, ed. Lamin Sanneh and Joel A. Carpenter (Oxford: Oxford University Press, 2005), 81–96.

10 Eddie Gibbs and Ryan K. Bolger, *Emerging Churches* (Grand Rapids: Baker, 2005), 235.

11 Wilbert R. Shenk, "Contextual Theology: The Last Frontier," in *The Changing Face of Christianity*, ed. Lamin Sanneh and Joel A. Carpenter, 191.

12 Sharyl Corrado and Toivo Pilli, eds., *Eastern European Baptist History: New Perspectives* (Prague: International Baptist Theological Seminary, 2007), 7.

13 Corrado and Pilli, 8–11.

14 Dietrich Bonhoeffer, "By Gracious Powers," in *Baptist Praise and Worship* (Oxford: Oxford University Press, 1991), 175; emphasis added.

Chapter 2

1   William Warren Sweet, *Religion in the Development of American Culture 1765–1840* (New York: Charles Scribner's Sons, 1952), 158.

2   Robert Torbet, *A History of the Baptists*, 3rd ed. (Valley Forge, Pa.: Judson, 1963), 18–21.

3   Torbet, 21–29.

4   William Lumpkin, *Baptist Confessions of Faith*, rev. ed. (Valley Forge, Pa.: Judson, 1969), 224. The Confession of 1660 begins, "A brief confession or declaration of faith set forth by many of us, who are (falsely) called Anabaptists. . . ."

5   Torbet, 29–37.

6   Bill J. Leonard, *Baptist Ways: A History* (Valley Forge, Pa.: Judson, 2003), 183–85.

7   William Whitsitt, *A Question in Baptist History* (New York: Arno, 1980), 89.

8   Whitsitt, 15.

9   Thomas R. McKibbens, "The Life, Writings, and Influence of Morgan Edwards," *Quarterly Review* 11 (1976): 68.

10   Sidney Mead, *The Lively Experiment* (New York: Harper & Row, 1963), 108.

11   Charles Reagan Wilson, *Baptized in Blood: The Religion of the Lost Cause* (Athens: University of Georgia Press, 1980).

12   Bill J. Leonard, *God's Last and Only Hope: The Fragmentation of the Southern Baptist Convention* (Grand Rapids: Eerdmans, 1990), 13.

13   *Alabama Christian Advocate*, June 29, 1948; and Leonard, *God's Last and Only Hope*, vi.

14   Robert A. Baker, *The Southern Baptist Convention and Its People, 1607–1972* (Nashville: Broadman, 1972), 154.

15   See John Lee Eighmy, *Churches in Cultural Captivity* (Knoxville: University of Tennessee Press, 1987); Rufus Spain, *At Ease in Zion* (Nashville: Vanderbilt University Press, 1967); and Samuel S. Hill Jr., *Southern Churches in Crisis* (New York: Holt, Rinehart, & Winston, 1967).

16   James L. Peacock and Ruel W. Tyson Jr., *Pilgrims of Paradox: Calvinism and Experience among the Primitive Baptists of the Blue Ridge* (Washington, D.C.: Smithsonian Institution Press, 1989), 6.

17   Paul Harvey, *Redeeming the South: Religious, Social and Cultural Identities among Southern Baptists, 1845–1925* (Chapel Hill: University of North Carolina Press, 1997), 4.

18   Steven R. Harmon, *Towards Baptist Catholicity: Essays on Tradition and the Baptist Vision* (Waynesboro, Ga.: Paternoster, 2006), 34.

19   Harmon, 37. *see* also Curtis Freeman, "A Confession for Catholic Baptists," in *Ties That Bind: Life Together in the Baptist Vision*, ed. G. Furr and C. W. Freeman (Macon, Ga.: Smyth & Helwys, 1994), 94.

20   Richard Quebedeaux, *The Worldly Evangelicals* (San Francisco: Harper & Row, 1978).

21   Harvey, 4.

Chapter 3

1   Lumpkin, 120.

2   Henry Cook, *What Baptists Stand For* (London: Kingsgate Press, 1947),

cited in Brian Stanley, "Planting Self-Governing Churches," *Baptist Quarterly* 34 (1992): 66.

3   Christine Leigh Heyrman, *Southern Cross: The Beginnings of the Bible Belt* (New York: Knopf, 1997), 97.

4   B. R. White, *The English Baptists of the Seventeenth Century*, rev. ed. (Didcot, UK: Baptist Historical Society, 1996), 17–18; *see* also Leonard, *Baptist Ways*, 24–26.

5   Lumpkin, 120.

6   Paul S. Fiddes, "'Walking Together': The Place of Covenant Theology in Baptist Life Yesterday and Today," in *Pilgrim Pathways: Essays in Baptist History in Honour of B. R. White*, ed. William H. Brackney and Paul S. Fiddes (Macon, Ga.: Mercer University Press, 1999), 48.

7   Fiddes, "'Walking Together,'" 53–55; *see* also Leonard, *Baptist Ways*, 44–45.

8   Karen Smith, "The Covenant Life of Some Eighteenth-Century Calvinistic Baptists in Hampshire and Wilshire," in Brackney and Fiddes, *Pilgrim Pathways*, 168.

9   Lumpkin, 165–66.

10 Lumpkin, 168.

11 Lumpkin, 121–22.

12 Leonard, *Baptist Ways*, 28.

13 Leonard, *Baptist Ways*, 55.

14 Lumpkin, 168–69.

15 W. T. Whitley, *A History of British Baptists*, rev. ed. (London: Kingsgate, 1932), 86.

16 Lumpkin, 289.

17 H. Leon McBeth, *Sourcebook for the Baptist Heritage* (Nashville: Broadman, 1990), 216; *see* also Leonard, *Baptist Ways*, 170.

18 McBeth, *Sourcebook*, 220.

19 Walter Rauschenbusch, "Why I Am a Baptist," in *Baptists and the American Republic*, ed. J. M. Dawson (Nashville: Broadman, 1956), 173.

Chapter 4

1   John Smyth, *Differences of the Churches of the Separation*, 1608, reprinted in W. T. Whitley, ed., *The Works of John Smyth*, 2 vols. (Cambridge: Cambridge University Press, 1915), 1:269–70, in McBeth, *Sourcebook*, 14.

2   B. Keach, "From My House Near Horselydown, Southward," April 3, 1691, in McBeth, *Sourcebook*, 67.

3   "A Declaration of Faith of English People Remaining at Amsterdam in Holland," 1611, in Lumpkin, 122.

4 "The Confession of Faith, of Those Churches Which Are Commonly (though Falsely) Called Anabaptists," 1644, in Lumpkin, 158.

5 "An Orthodox Creed, or A Protestant Confession of Faith," 1679, in Lumpkin, 325.

6 "An Orthodox Creed," in Lumpkin, 325.

7 Lumpkin, 251.

8 David S. Dockery, *The Doctrine of the Bible* (Nashville: Convention Press, 1991), 81.

9 Dockery, 86. Dockery lists various books that affirm these varied approaches, including John R. Rice, *Our God-Breathed Book, the Bible* (Murfreesboro, Tenn.: Sword of the Lord Press, 1969); Harold Lindsell, *The Battle for the Bible* (Grand Rapids: Zondervan, 1976); Carl F. H. Henry, *God, Revelation, and Authority*, vol. 4 (Waco, Tex.: Word Books, 1981); and Clark H. Pinnock, *The Scripture Principle* (New York: Harper & Row, 1884). *see* also L. Russ Bush and Tom J. Nettles, *Baptists and the Bible* (Chicago: Moody, 1980).

10 Walter Harrelson, "Passing On the Biblical Tradition Intact: The Role of Historical Criticism," in *Beyond the Impasse? Scripture, Interpretation, & Theology in Baptist Life*, ed. Robison B. James and David S. Dockery (Nashville: Broadman, 1992), 41.

11 Molly Truman Marshall, "Setting Our Feet in a Large Room," in James and Dockery, *Beyond the Impasse*, 188.

12 See Harmon; Paul Fiddes, *Tracks and Traces: Baptist Identity in Church and Theology* (Waynesboro, Ga.: Paternoster, 2003); and C. Douglas Weaver, *In Search of the New Testament Church: The Baptist Story* (Macon, Ga.: Mercer University Press, 2008).

13 Beth Allison Barr, Bill J. Leonard, Mikeal C. Parsons, and C. Douglas Weaver, eds., *The Acts of the Apostles: Four Centuries of Baptist Interpretation* (Waco, Tex.: Baylor University Press, 2009).

14 Weaver, 10.

15 David Tracy, *Plurality and Ambiguity: Hermeneutics, Religion, Hope* (New York: Harper & Row, 1987), 14–15.

16 Lumpkin, 118.

17 Lumpkin, 162. *see* also 1 John 15:13; Rom 8:32-34; Rom 5:11, 3:25; Eph 2:8; John 6:29, 4:10; Phil 1:29; Gal 5:22.

18 Lumpkin, 330–31. Scriptures cited include Isa 7:16, 8:4; 2 Sam 12:19ff; Ezek 28:4ff; 1 Kgs 14:13; Matt 18:2-4; Jer 31:29-30; Deut 1:39; Matt 19:13-14; Mark 10:13ff.

19 Lumpkin, 265. The texts are John 3:3-6, 3:8.

20 Leonard, *Baptist Ways*, 104–5.

21 Leonard, *Baptist Ways*, 104.

22 Lumpkin, 265.

23 B. L. Beebe, comp., *The Feast of Fat Things* (Middletown, N.Y.: G. Beebe's Son, n.d.), 3–4.

24 Lumpkin, 364.

25 Randy J. Sparks, "Religion in Amite County, Mississippi, 1800–1861," in *Masters and Slaves in the House of the Lord: Race and Religion in the American South, 1740–1870*, ed. John B. Boles (Lexington: University Press of Kentucky, 1988), 68; also Leonard, *God's Last and Only Hope*, 21.

26 Larry E. Tise, *Proslavery: A History of the Defense of Slavery in America, 1701–1840* (Athens: University of Georgia Press, 1987), 39.

27 Richard Furman, *An Exposition*, 1822, in Bill J. Leonard, *Early American Christianity* (Nashville: Broadman, 1983), 382–83.

28 Tise, 40.

29 Tise, 105, 118.

30 David Barrow, *Involuntary, Unmerited, Perpetual, Absolute, Hereditary Slavery Examined, on the Principles of Nature, Reason, Justice, Policy and Scripture* (Lexington: D. C. Bradford, 1808), 30–31, 40–41, in *Baptist Life and Thought: 1600–1980*, ed. William H. Brackney (Valley Forge, Pa.: Judson, 1983), 145.

31 Richard Furman and Francis Wayland, *Domestic Slavery Considered as a Scriptural Institution* (New York: Lewis Colby, 1845), 9.

32 William Warren Sweet, *Religion on the American Frontier: The Baptists 1780–1830* (Chicago: University of Chicago Press, 1931), 328–29.

33 Sweet, 330.

34 Bill J. Leonard, *Baptists in America* (New York: Columbia University Press, 2005), 220.

35 www.sbc.net/bfm/bfm2000.asp.

36 Carolyn D. Blevins, *Women's Place in Baptist Life* (Brentwood, Tenn.: Baptist History and Heritage Society, 2003), 13; and Leonard, *Baptists in America*, 215.

37 Sarah F. Ward, "Woman's Christian Temperance Union," *Criswell Theological Journal* 5, no. 2 (2008): 53–70; and Richard Land and Barrett Duke, "The Christian and Alcohol," *Criswell Theological Journal* 5, no. 2 (2008): 19–38.

38 Frederic Richard Lees and Dawson Burns, *The Temperance Bible-Commentary* (London: S. W. Partridge, 1868), 304–5, cited in Land and Duke, 32n15.

39 M. E. Dodd, *Baptist Principles* (Alexandria, La.: Chronicle, 1916), 79.

40   Crowley, 180; and Bill J. Leonard, "'They Have No Wine': Wet/Dry Bap-
     tists and the Alcohol Issues," *Criswell Theological Journal* 5, no. 2 (2008):
     3–17.

Chapter 5

1   "A Declaration of Faith of English People Remaining in Amsterdam in Hol-
     land," in Lumpkin, 119.
2   Frederick Buechner, *The Sacred Journey* (New York: Harper & Row, 1982),
     109.
3   William James, *The Varieties of Religious Experience* (New York: Modern
     Library, 1929), 79.
4   Martin Luther, *Ninety-Five Theses*, in Henry Bettenson, *Documents of the
     Christian Church* (Oxford: Oxford University Press, 1963), 263.
5   Martin Luther, *On the Babylonish Captivity of the Church*, in Bettenson, *Docu-
     ments of the Christian Church*, 279.
6   John Calvin, *The Institutes of the Christian Religion*, vol. 1 (Edinburgh: T&T
     Clark, 1863), 257.
7   Calvin, 255.
8   Sydney Ahlstrom, *A Religious History of the American People* (New Haven:
     Yale University Press, 1972), 128.
9   Ahlstrom, 132.
10   "The Standard Confession," 1660, in Lumpkin, 226–27; *see* also Fiddes,
     Tracks and Traces, 229.
11   "The Orthodox Creed," 1679, in Lumpkin, 316.
12   Lumpkin, 230.
13   "Second London Confession," 1677/1688, in Lumpkin, 268–69.
14   Lumpkin, 272–73.
15   Jonathan Edwards, *A Faithful Narrative of the Surprising Work of God* (1735),
     in *Early American Religion*, ed. Bill J. Leonard (Nashville: Broadman, 1983),
     203.
16   Edwards, 237.
17   Edwards, 203–8.
18   Charles G. Finney, *Lectures on Revivals of Religion* (New York: Fleming H.
     Revell, 1888), 355.
19   David Benedict, *A General History of the Baptist Denomination in America*, 2
     vols. (Boston: Manning & Loring, 1813), 1:251, in McBeth, *Sourcebook*,
     167.
20   Harvey, 117.
21   Harvey, 117.
22   R. A. Torrey, *How to Promote and Conduct a Successful Revival* (New York:

Fleming H. Revell, 1901), 167; *see* also Bill J. Leonard, "Getting Saved in America: Conversion Event in a Pluralistic Culture," in *Out of One, Many: American Religion and American Pluralism* (DeLand, Fla.: Stetson University, 1984), 12.

23 See www.av1611.org/etern.

24 Curtis Mitchell, *Those Who Came Forward* (Philadelphia: Chilton, 1966), 5; also Leonard, "Getting Saved in America," 12.

25 Samuel Hill and Dennis Owen, *The New Political Religious Right in America* (Nashville: Abingdon, 1982), 122.

26 "First London Confession," 1644, in Lumpkin, 163.

27 Lumpkin, 273–74.

28 See www.av1611.org/etern.

29 Gibbs and Bolger, 63.

30 Gibbs and Bolger, 56; emphasis in original.

31 Lumpkin, 119.

32 Lumpkin, 318.

Chapter 6

1 Daniel Featley, *The Dippers Dipt, or, the Anabaptists Duck'd and Plung'd over Head and Eares, at a Disputation at Southward*, 36.

2 Isaac Backus, *Church History of New England, from 1620 to 1804* (Philadelphia: American Baptist Publication Society, 1844), 43.

3 Isaac Backus, *A History of New England, with Particular Reference to the Baptists*, 2nd ed. (1871; repr., 2 vols., New York: Arno, 1969), 1:75.

4 Lumpkin, 331–32.

5 Lumpkin, 120.

6 Lumpkin, 120.

7 Lumpkin, 119.

8 Lumpkin, 233.

9 Maria Bonafede, "The Responsibilities of a Minority," typescript, e-mail to Bill J. Leonard, June 30, 2008.

Chapter 7

1 "Southern Baptist Leaders Disagree: Can Retooling Reverse Decline?" *USA Today*, June 22, 2009; and "Structure Proposal Defeated," *American Baptist News Service*, July 7, 2009.

2 H. Leon McBeth, *The Baptist Heritage* (Nashville: Broadman, 1987), 347–50.

3 Phyllis Tickle, *The Great Emergence* (Grand Rapids: Baker, 2008), 150–51.

4   Tickle, 152–53.
5   Lumpkin, 119.
6   Lumpkin, 120.
7   Anthony R. Cross, *Baptism and the Baptists: Theology and Practice in Twentieth Century Britain* (Waynesboro, Ga.: Paternoster, 2000), 1–2.
8   Cross, 455.
9   Cross, 456–57.
10   Cross, 458–59.
11   Lumpkin, 120.
12   Lumpkin, 120.
13   Fiddes, *Tracks and Traces*, 77–78; emphasis in original.
14   Lumpkin, 122.
15   Lumpkin, 120.

BIBLIOGRAPHY

Ahlstrom, Sydney. *A Religious History of the American People*. New Haven: Yale University Press, 1972.

Alabama Christian Advocate. June 29, 1948.

Backus, Isaac. *Church History of New England, from 1620 to 1804*. Philadelphia: American Baptist Publication Society, 1844.

————. *A History of New England, with Particular Reference to the Baptists*. 1871. 2 vols., 2nd ed. Reprint, New York: Arno, 1969.

Baker, Robert A. *The Southern Baptist Convention and Its People, 1607–1972*. Nashville: Broadman, 1972.

Barr, Beth Allison, Bill J. Leonard, Mikeal C. Parsons, and C. Douglas Weaver, eds. *The Acts of the Apostles: Four Centuries of Baptist Interpretation*. Waco, Tex.: Baylor University Press, 2009.

Barrow, David. *Involuntary, Unmerited, Perpetual, Absolute, Hereditary Slavery Examined, on the Principles of Nature, Reason, Justice, Policy and Scripture*. Lexington: D. C. Bradford, 1808.

Beebe, B. L., comp. *The Feast of Fat Things*. Middletown, N.Y.: G. Beebe's Son, n.d.

Benedict, David. *A General History of the Baptist Denomination in America*. 2 vols. Boston: Manning & Loring, 1813.

Bettenson, Henry. *Documents of the Christian Church*. Oxford: Oxford University Press, 1963.

Blevins, Carolyn D. *Women's Place in Baptist Life*. Brentwood, Tenn.: Baptist History and Heritage Society, 2003.

Bonhoeffer, Dietrich. "By Gracious Powers." In *Baptist Praise and Worship*, 175. Oxford: Oxford University Press, 1991.

Brackney, William H., ed. *Baptist Life and Thought: 1600–1980*. Valley Forge, Pa.: Judson, 1983.

Brackney, William H., and Paul S. Fiddes, eds. *Pilgrim Pathways: Essays in Baptist History in Honour of B. R. White*. Macon, Ga.: Mercer University Press, 1999.

Buechner, Frederick. *The Sacred Journey*. New York: Harper & Row, 1982.

Bush, L. Russ, and Tom J. Nettles. *Baptists and the Bible*. Chicago: Moody, 1980.

Calvin, John. *The Institutes of the Christian Religion*. Vol. 1. Edinburgh: T&T Clark, 1863.

"The Confession of Faith, of Those Churches Which Are Commonly (though Falsely) Called Anabaptists." 1644. In Lumpkin, *Baptist Confessions*, 158.

Cook, Henry. *What Baptists Stand For*. London: Kingsgate Press, 1947.

Corrado, Sharyl, and Toivo Pilli, eds. *Eastern European Baptist History: New Perspectives*. Prague: International Baptist Theological Seminary, 2007.

Cross, Anthony R. *Baptism and the Baptists: Theology and Practice in Twentieth Century Britain*. Waynesboro, Ga.: Paternoster, 2000.

Crowley, John G. *Primitive Baptists of the Wiregrass South 1815 to the Present*. Gainesville: University of Florida Press, 1998.

"A Declaration of Faith of English People Remaining at Amsterdam in Holland." 1611. In Lumpkin, *Baptist Confessions*, 122.

Dockery, David S. *The Doctrine of the Bible*. Nashville: Convention Press, 1991.

Dodd, M. E. *Baptist Principles*. Alexandria, La.: Chronicle, 1916.

Edwards, Jonathan. *A Faithful Narrative of the Surprising Work of God*. In *Early American Religion*, edited by Bill J. Leonard, 203. Nashville: Broadman, 1983.

Featley, Daniel. *The Dippers Dipt, or, the Anabaptists Duck'd and Plung'd over Head and Eares, at a Disputation at Southward*.

Fiddes, Paul. *Tracks and Traces: Baptist Identity in Church and Theology*. Waynesboro, Ga.: Paternoster, 2003.

————. "'Walking Together': The Place of Covenant Theology in Baptist Life Yesterday and Today." In Brackney and Fiddes, *Pilgrim Pathways*, 47–74.

Finney, Charles G. *Lectures on Revivals of Religion*. New York: Fleming H. Revell, 1888.

"First London Confession." 1644. In Lumpkin, *Baptist Confessions*, 163.

Freeman, Curtis. "A Confession for Catholic Baptists." In *Ties That Bind: Life Together in the Baptist Vision*, edited by G. Furr and C. W. Freeman, 83–96. Macon, Ga.: Smyth & Helwys, 1994.

Furman, Richard. *An Exposition*. 1822. In *Early American Christianity*, by Bill J. Leonard, 382–83. Nashville: Broadman, 1983.

Furman, Richard, and Francis Wayland. *Domestic Slavery Considered as a Scriptural Institution*. New York: Lewis Colby, 1845.

Gibbs, Eddie, and Ryan K. Bolger. *Emerging Churches*. Grand Rapids: Baker, 2005.

Gifford, Paul. "A View of Ghana's New Christianity." In Sanneh and Carpenter, *The Changing Face of Christianity*, 81–96.

Harmon, Steven R. *Towards Baptist Catholicity: Essays on Tradition and the Baptist Vision*. Waynesboro, Ga.: Paternoster, 2006.

Harrelson, Walter. "Passing On the Biblical Tradition Intact: The Role of Historical Criticism." In James and Dockery, *Beyond the Impasse?* 41.

Harvey, Paul. *Redeeming the South: Religious, Social and Cultural Identities among Southern Baptists, 1845–1925*. Chapel Hill: University of North Carolina Press, 1997.

Henry, Carl F. H. *God, Revelation, and Authority.* Vol. 4. Waco, Tex.: Word Books, 1981.

Heyrman, Christine Leigh. *Southern Cross: The Beginnings of the Bible Belt.* New York: Knopf, 1997.

Hill, Christopher. *The World Turned Upside Down.* 1984. Reprint, New York: Penguin, 1991.

Hill, Samuel, and Dennis Owen. *The New Political Religious Right in America.* Nashville: Abingdon, 1982.

Hooker, Richard J., ed. *The Carolina Backcountry on the Eve of the Revolution: The Journal and Other Writings of Charles Woodmason, Anglican Itinerant.* Chapel Hill: University of North Carolina Press, 1953.

James, Robison B., and David S. Dockery, eds. *Beyond the Impasse? Scripture, Interpretation, & Theology in Baptist Life.* Nashville: Broadman, 1992.

James, William. *The Varieties of Religious Experience.* New York: Modern Library, 1929.

Keach, B. "From My House Near Horselydown, Southward." April 3, 1691. In McBeth, *Sourcebook,* 67.

Land, Richard, and Barrett Duke. "The Christian and Alcohol." *Criswell Theological Journal* 5, no. 2 (2008): 19–38.

Lees, Frederic Richard, and Dawson Burns. *The Temperance Bible-Commentary.* London: S. W. Partridge, 1868.

Leonard, Bill J. *Baptist Ways: A History.* Valley Forge, Pa.: Judson, 2003.

————. *Baptists in America.* New York: Columbia University Press, 2005.

————. "Getting Saved in America: Conversion Event in a Pluralistic Culture." In *Out of One, Many: American Religion and American Pluralism,* 12. DeLand, Fla.: Stetson University, 1984.

————. *God's Last and Only Hope: The Fragmentation of the Southern Baptist Convention.* Grand Rapids: Eerdmans, 1990.

————. "'They Have No Wine': Wet/Dry Baptists and the Alcohol Issues." *Criswell Theological Journal* 5, no. 2 (2008): 3–17.

Lindsell, Harold. *The Battle for the Bible*. Grand Rapids: Zondervan, 1976.

Lumpkin, William. *Baptist Confessions of Faith*. Rev. ed. Valley Forge, Pa.: Judson, 1969.

Luther, Martin. *Ninety-Five Theses*. In Bettenson, *Documents of the Christian Church*, 263.

―――. *On the Babylonish Captivity of the Church*. In Bettenson, *Documents of the Christian Church*, 279.

Marshall, Molly Truman. "Setting Our Feet in a Large Room." In James and Dockery, *Beyond the Impasse?* 188.

McBeth, H. Leon. *The Baptist Heritage*. Nashville: Broadman, 1987.

―――. *Sourcebook for the Baptist Heritage*. Nashville: Broadman, 1990.

McKibbens, Thomas R. "The Life, Writings, and Influence of Morgan Edwards." *Quarterly Review* 11 (1976): 68.

Mead, Sidney. *The Lively Experiment*. New York: Harper & Row, 1963.

Mitchell, Curtis. *Those Who Came Forward*. Philadelphia: Chilton, 1966.

"An Orthodox Creed, or A Protestant Confession of Faith." 1679. In Lumpkin, *Baptist Confessions*, 325.

Peacock, James L., and Ruel W. Tyson Jr. *Pilgrims of Paradox: Calvinism and Experience among the Primitive Baptists of the Blue Ridge*. Washington, D.C.: Smithsonian Institution Press, 1989.

Pinnock, Clark H. *The Scripture Principle*. New York: Harper & Row, 1884.

Rauschenbusch, Walter. "Why I Am a Baptist." In *Baptists and the American Republic*, edited by J. M. Dawson, 173. Nashville: Broadman, 1956.

Rice, John R. *Our God-Breathed Book, the Bible*. Murfreesboro, Tenn.: Sword of the Lord Press, 1969.

Sanneh, Lamin, and Joel A. Carpenter, eds. *The Changing Face of*

Christianity: Africa, the West, and the World. Oxford: Oxford University Press, 2005.

"Second London Confession." 1677/1688. In Lumpkin, *Baptist Confessions*, 268–69.

Shenk, Wilbert R. "Contextual Theology: The Last Frontier." In Sanneh and Carpenter, *The Changing Face of Christianity*, 191–205.

Smith, Karen. "The Covenant Life of Some Eighteenth-Century Calvinistic Baptists in Hampshire and Wilshire." In Brackney and Fiddes, *Pilgrim Pathways*, 168.

Smyth, John. *Differences of the Churches of the Separation.* 1608. Reprinted in *The Works of John Smyth*, edited by W. T. Whitley. 2 vols. Cambridge: Cambridge University Press, 1915.

"Southern Baptist Leaders Disagree: Can Retooling Reverse Decline?" *USA Today*, June 22, 2009.

Sparks, Randy J. "Religion in Amite County, Mississippi, 1800–1861." In *Masters and Slaves in the House of the Lord: Race and Religion in the American South, 1740–1870*, edited by John B. Boles, 58–80. Lexington: University Press of Kentucky, 1988.

"The Standard Confession." 1660. In Lumpkin, *Baptist Confessions*, 226–27.

Stanley, Brian. "Planting Self-Governing Churches." *Baptist Quarterly* 34 (1992): 66.

"Structure Proposal Defeated." *American Baptist News Service*, July 7, 2009.

Sweet, William Warren. *Religion on the American Frontier: The Baptists 1780–1830.* Chicago: University of Chicago Press, 1931.

Tickle, Phyllis. *The Great Emergence.* Grand Rapids: Baker, 2008.

Tise, Larry E. *Proslavery: A History of the Defense of Slavery in America, 1701–1840.* Athens: University of Georgia Press, 1987.

Torbet, Robert. *A History of the Baptists.* 3rd ed. Valley Forge, Pa.: Judson, 1963.

Torrey, R. A. *How to Promote and Conduct a Successful Revival.* New York: Fleming H. Revell, 1901.

Tracy, David. *Plurality and Ambiguity: Hermeneutics, Religion, Hope.* New York: Harper & Row, 1987.

Turley, Jonathan. "Minister Prays for Death of President Obama." JonathanTurley.org. June 5, 2009.

"Va. Congressman Fears More Muslims Elected." www.msnbc. msn.com/id/16311648, December 21, 2006.

Ward, Sarah F. "Woman's Christian Temperance Union." *Criswell Theological Journal* 5, no. 2 (2008): 53–70.

Weaver, C. Douglas. *In Search of the New Testament Church: The Baptist Story.* Macon, Ga.: Mercer University Press, 2008.

White, B. R. *The English Baptists of the Seventeenth Century.* Rev. ed. Didcot, UK: Baptist Historical Society, 1996.

Whitley, W. T. *A History of British Baptists.* Rev. ed. London: Kingsgate, 1932.

Whitsitt, William. *A Question in Baptist History.* New York: Arno, 1980.

Wilson, Charles Reagan. *Baptized in Blood: The Religion of the Lost Cause.* Athens: University of Georgia Press, 1980.

INDEX OF AUTHORS

SUBJECT INDEX